"A new series that promises to blend scholarly research with popular appeal....comprehensive, authoritative,...excellent references."

—Clarence Petersen,
Chicago Tribune

Bantam/Britannica Books

**Unique, authoritative guides
to acquiring human knowledge**

What motivates people and nations? What makes things work? What laws and history lie behind the strivings and conflicts of contemporary man?

One of mankind's greatest natural endowments is the urge to learn. Bantam/Britannica books were created to help make that goal a reality. Distilled and edited from the vast Britannica files, these compact introductory volumes offer uniquely accessible summaries of human knowledge. Technology and science, politics, natural disasters, world events—just about everything that the inquisitive person wants to know about is fully explained and explored.

BANTAM/BRITANNICA BOOKS

Law in America

How and Why It Works

**Prepared by
the Editors of
Encyclopaedia
Britannica**

The Encyclopaedia Britannica staff for
BANTAM/BRITANNICA BOOKS

Editor	Frank Gibney
Executive Editor	Richard Pope

LAW IN AMERICA: HOW AND WHY IT WORKS

Subject Editor	Dennis J. Hutchinson
Editorial Assistant	Celeste McManman
Art Director	Cynthia Peterson
Picture Editor	Holly Harrington
Layout Artist	Richard Batchelor
Editorial Production Manager	J. Thomas Beatty
Production Coordinator	Elizabeth A. Blowers
Index Supervisor	Frances E. Latham
Indexers	Anthony M. Mariella
	Mary Neumann

Encyclopaedia Britannica, Inc.

Chairman of the Board	Robert P. Gwinn
President	Charles E. Swanson

Foreword:
Knowledge for Today's World

One of mankind's greatest natural endowments is the urge to learn. Whether we call it knowledge-seeking, intellectual curiosity, or plain nosiness, most people feel a need to get behind the newspaper page or the TV newscast and seek out the background events: What motivates people and nations? What makes things work? How is science explained? What laws and history lie behind the strivings and conflicts of contemporary man? Yet the very richness of information that bombards us daily often makes it hard to acquire such knowledge, given with authority, about the forces and factors influencing our lives.

The editors at Britannica have spent a great deal of time, over the years, pondering this problem. Their ultimate answer, the 15th Edition of the *Encyclopaedia Britannica*, has been lauded not merely as a vast, comprehensive collection of information but also as a unique, informed summary of human knowledge in an orderly and innovative form. Besides this work, they have also thought to produce a series of compact introductory volumes providing essential information about a wide variety of peoples and problems, cultures, crafts, and disciplines. Hence the birth of these Bantam/Britannica books.

The Bantam/Britannica books, prepared under the guidance of the Britannica's Board of Editors, have been distilled and edited from the vast repository of information in the Britannica archives. The editors have also used the mine of material in the 14th Edition, a great work in its own right, which is no longer being published because much of its material did not fit the design imposed by the 15th. In addition to these sources, current Britannica files and reports—including those for annual yearbooks and for publications in other languages—were made available for this new series.

All of the Bantam/Britannica books are prepared by Britannica editors in our Chicago headquarters with the assistance of specialized subject editors for some volumes. The Bantam/Britannica books cover the widest possible range of topics. They are current and contemporary as well as cultural and historical. They are designed to provide *knowledge for today*—for students anxious to grasp the essentials of a subject, for concerned citizens who want to know more about how their world works, for the intellectually curious who like good reading in concise form. They are a stepping stone to the thirty-volume *Encyclopaedia Britannica*, not a substitute for it. That is why references to the 15th Edition, also known as *Britannica 3* because of its three distinct parts, are included in the bibliographies. While additional research is always recommended, these books are complete unto themselves. Just about everything that the inquisitive person needs to catch up on a subject is contained within their pages. They make good companions, as well as good teachers. Read them.

The Editors,
Encyclopaedia Britannica

Contents

Introduction:
Seams in the Web

No one, layman or lawyer, finds the U.S. legal system easy to understand. Unlike some countries, the United States does not have a nationally uniform body of law that applies throughout the country in all circumstances. The explanation for the complexity of U.S. law is, of course, the fiercely "federal" nature of the Constitution, which divides duties, sometimes unclearly, between the national and state or local governments.

The purpose of *Law in America* is to describe the development of the American legal system and to discuss the tension that exists between state and federal power. The book is a survey of where American law came from and what it is today. It is not intended to be a "how to" book or to serve as a "paperback lawyer." Instead, *Law in America* describes U.S. law by placing it in historical perspective.

A survey of American law, or of any general body of law, must inevitably make arbitrary, if not artificial, distinctions. It was once popular to say that the law is a "seamless web." Actually, the more closely the law is examined, the more seams appear. Legal problems, however, do not fall neatly into simple categories such as "tort" or "contract." They tend instead to involve numerous principles, many of which overlap. Dividing our body of law into categories does, however, provide a convenient frame of reference for anyone who wants to begin to understand the breadth and detail of our legal system.

Law in America is divided into five main sections. Part I is a general history of the development of the American legal system, including a discussion of the impulse to codify.

Parts II, III, and IV survey specific areas of law from several perspectives: The individual and the Constitution; business and corporate and other specialized laws; the private citizen and so-called common law and other regulations of private transactions and behavior; and "administrative law," the law that affects the various agencies that—taken as a whole—add up to what many people call "big government." Included is a discussion of a unique feature of U.S. law—the power of "judicial review." No other country tolerates as much power in the hands of its judges or locates the source of that power implicitly in a written constitution, facts that profoundly influence the nature of our law.

Part V offers a brief sketch of the personnel of American law—the bench and the bar. It also includes discussions of legal education and of legal aid.

Although *Law in America* attempts to explain the fundamentals of the U.S. legal system, it cannot claim to be exhaustive. The complexities of our system of law—the work of generations of American jurists, lawyers, and legislators—are simply too great for one book. *Law in America* does, however, offer an account of the origins and development of our legal system, as well as an idea of its pervasive influence on our lives today.

I. History of the Legal System

"The law is the last result of human wisdom acting upon human experience for the benefit of the public."

—Samuel Johnson

1.
Common Law and the Courts

In a strictly technical sense, there is no such thing as "American law." The reason is institutional: apart from the Constitution, there is no national supreme tribunal to unify legal doctrine. Moreover, the United States as a sovereign body has no national "common law"—a body of rules and principles, based on judicial decisions and developed over a long period of time. Each state has its own common law, which is unrestrained other than by certain provisions of the federal Constitution. The result is a crazy quilt of different rules, principles, and requirements from state to state, with little unity of effect or philosophy.

For more than a century (until only a generation ago) unity of legal doctrine was thought to be both desirable and achievable. The chief instrument for its promotion was the power of the federal courts (circuit, district, and claims) to develop an independent body of national doctrine in the field of general commercial law. The uniformity produced, however, was more illusory than real. Partly because of disappointment in the degree of uniformity achieved and partly because of a more general philosophical change, the Supreme Court nullified the lower federal courts' power in that area in the case of *Erie R.R. Co.* v. *Tompkins* (1938). In place of a national common law the Supreme Court required the lower courts to apply the law of the state in such cases. The general primacy of state law as opposed to national common law was thereby reestablished.

The goal of national uniformity, however, was not discarded at a stroke. Two highly significant but less conspicuous forces remained at work: the National Conference of Commissioners on Uniform State Laws and the American Law Institute (ALI). The National Conference has developed codes and model laws for adoption by the states. Its greatest triumph was the Uniform Commercial Code, which by 1968 was law in every state but Louisiana (originally a French territory, which uniquely retains the civil code established by the French). The ALI has been somewhat less influential, although its "restatements" of the law in several substantive areas have helped reshape academic and professional thought. In short, while national uniformity has always been more a goal than a reality it has always been a force in the American legal system. The growth of uniformity mirrors—at least in a sense—the growth of the legal system itself and can be divided into four major periods of development: pre-1776, 1776–1828, 1828–1868, and post-1868.

Before 1776

It is a traditional judicial article of faith that the colonists brought with them, almost as a birthright, the English common law—its concepts of liberty, property, and justice and such of its technical rules as fitted colonial conditions. Although the colonists did claim the "rights of Englishmen," they neither claimed nor desired the bulk of the English common law. Apparently they felt that it was part and parcel of an oppressive imperial government. All of the New England colonies, for example, denied that the English common law was binding. And although half a dozen other colonies tried, after a fashion, to follow it, they had their own codes of law to cover their basic needs. Some of the codes were extraordinarily detailed and complete. As a result, the English common law became subsidiary. In fact, only three colonies gave explicit statutory recognition to English law during the colonial period. (Later, in the post-colonial period, Americans turned to the English common law as a basis for creating law that would serve the new country.)

In addition, the colonies were geographically isolated and British imperial control was slight. The colonists were free, particularly during the seventeenth century, to experiment in law. Dozens of striking innovations that seem singularly modern to us were imposed upon the common law. Some even persisted into later law.

The history of the period is more interesting than important, however. In the first place the practices and procedures developed were both too divergent from the common law and too informal to take hold permanently. Two drawbacks were the lack of lawbooks—original, reprinted, or imported—and the shortage of professionally trained lawyers. Even the chief justices were rarely lawyers. Without printed laws or codes and without technically trained professionals to give the system some degree of formality, the law of the early colonial period was basically a system of lay persons distributing natural equity, or the law of justice that prevails between one person and another.

In the eighteenth century something resembling indepen-

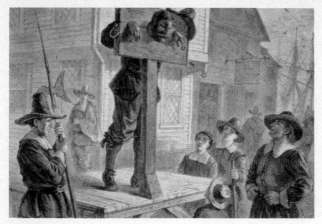

With the shortage of professional lawyers during the colonial period, the law was often an informal system with lay persons or groups passing judgment on their peers.

dent judicial courts developed, but with them came the English common law, as imperial control of the colonies tightened. About four hundred colonial statutes (laws enacted by legislative assemblies) were simply disallowed by the Crown because they deviated from common law. Judicial appeals to England grew steadily more numerous. A professional bar—an organization of practicing lawyers, for which there had evidently been no place in the preceding century—gradually developed. Many of its leaders (perhaps 50 before 1760, and about 115 between 1760 and 1783) were products of the Inns of Court in England. But most were simply graduates of American colleges who then "read law" (studied in the office of a lawyer) until they were ready to practice.

This period was one of absorption of the English law. It was marked by the disappearance of the older colonial innovations and the development of a few new practices. A striking feature of the evolving system was the persistence of numerous local tribunals that brought justice nearer to every person.

English common law, however, was not adopted uniformly. Certain colonial conditions made English doctrinal notions irrelevant or superfluous. On a more subtle level, the mere transfer of law doctrine and custom from one country to another often resulted in the loss of doctrinal baggage along the way: "mere ignorance had freed the colonies of a great mass of antiquated and useless rubbish."

From 1776 to 1828

During the period from the Revolution to the era of Andrew Jackson, Americans continued to adopt the English common law as the basis of law in the United States, but only as it suited the American conditions. This continued to be a period of reception of English law, rather than a time of development of wholly separate native institutions, although courts of equity provided some remedies where English law failed. But there was still no separate body of American law. The first volume of "American reports" (published American judicial decisions) did not appear until 1789, and less than a dozen volumes were in print by 1800. This lack is more than a grace note of the period, for without printed books detailing laws and judicial opinions there was no customary law in the sense that we have come to think of it—that is, ascertainable rules on which lawyers and laymen could rely for advice on liability and for settling disputes. Indeed, when law professor James Kent of Columbia College in New York City was appointed to the New York Supreme Court in 1798, there were still no case reports for that state.

Kent greatly influenced American legal development. "English authority," he wrote, "did not stand very high in these early feverish times, and this led me a hundred times to bear down opposition or shame it by exhaustive research and overwhelming authority." Kent's "researches" became a cornerstone of the emerging American legal system. Free from hampering precedents, in his twenty-five years as a judge he gave form to the entire law of New York. In the process he also made an unrivaled contribution to the law of the whole country through his *Commentaries* (1826–30). It is generally agreed that they are worthy of comparison with the famous works of Sir William Blackstone written earlier in the century in England. Kent set himself the task of establishing the common law by basing all decisions possible on it, and he succeeded. He valued certainty in the law over innovation and had none of the reformers' spirit. This is evidenced by his sigh over "the piles of learning" and "the profound logic, skilful criticism and refined distinctions" that were doomed to disuse after New York abolished an old and venerated rule of property law by enacting a restrictive statute.

Some basic statutes emerged during this period. They included: those laws granting powers over chattels to courts of equity; legitimizing children by subsequent marriage of the parents; and abolishing primogeniture (the rights of inheritance of the firstborn) and establishing inheritance equally by all children. Limited liability was conferred on corporations, and a general rule was provided under which corporations might organize freely.

As early as 1776 Pennsylvania—"the first of civilized countries to do so"—provided in its constitution for a penitentiary where prisoners were to be segregated by sex and the severity of their offenses. At the same time the state introduced laws for the relief of insolvent debtors. In 1827 New York made a revision of its statute book, changing fundamentally the law

Through his decisions based on common law and his written commentaries, James Kent, a New York Supreme Court justice, greatly influenced the American legal system during its formative years.

State legislatures passed notable reform statutes during the period following the Revolution. In its constitution Pennsylvania provided for a penitentiary segregating offenders according to sex and the nature of their crimes.

of real property and, in effect, providing a model that was adopted later in several other states. Cases formerly dealt with under colonial laws that had fallen into disuse were provided for under new state laws. The experimental spirit of the state legislature was not mirrored in the judiciary, however. There were frequent complaints that judges woodenly applied rather technical rules at the expense of justice.

From 1828 to 1868

The triumph of frontier democracy, with Andrew Jackson's election to the presidency in 1828, marked the transition to a new era in politics and in the law. It was also a period of new inventions, such as the reaper and the steel plow. There was a land boom, and people spread west, beyond the Missouri River.

Although individualism ruled American society in politics and economics, the period was remarkable for its social and community spirit. More people were gaining the right to vote. Antislavery and other reform movements were being organized. Improvements in both judicial and legislative branches of the law reveal the period's originality as well. What Ameri-

As a law professor at Harvard University during the early nineteenth century, Supreme Court Justice Joseph Story published nine legal commentaries that had a profound effect on the emerging American legal system.

can legal scholar John H. Wigmore said much later of the law of evidence could be said of other fields of law: "Partly because of the lack of treatises and reports, partly because of the tendency to question important rules and therefore to defend on grounds of principle and policy whatever could be defended, partly because of the moral obligation of the judiciary, in new communities, to vindicate by intellectual effort its right to supremacy over the bar, and partly, also, because of the advent, coincidentally, of the same rationalizing spirit which led to the reformatory legislation—this very necessity of restatement led to a finely reasoned system."

Important in this period, rivaling the influence of Kent in the preceding period, was the work of the American jurist Joseph Story. In thirteen years (1832–45) he published nine remarkable textbooks, which in succeeding editions had a profound effect on forming American law. Thus, in the law of evidence, "the period from 1840 to 1870 saw the enactment, in the various jurisdictions of this country, of most of the reformatory legislation which had been carried or proposed in England," and the promulgation of a body of opinions "superior (on the whole) to the judgments uttered in the native home of our law."

As commerce grew and as the frontier rapidly expanded, courts had occasion to develop new doctrines adapted to a changing world. The expanding United States, with its wide variety of industries and activities, required a severe modification of the rules that had been created in England hundreds of years earlier to suit that small, agrarian country. For example, a remarkable adoption of frontier customs (though mainly by statute) was that of the mining and water laws developed in western mining camps.

The legislation of the period was even more distinctive than the work of the courts. For the first time, reform by statute became the primary characteristic of American government and law. According to Ernst Freund, author of *Standards of American Legislation* (1917), "The establishment of self-government on a new soil realized the idea of the people as the source of political power as it had not been realized in historic times." On a scale equally unique the people sought fervently to illustrate the dictum that democracy relies on laws and not on men. Religious and property qualifications for voting, officeholding, and jury services were swept away by the middle of the century, although sexual distinctions persisted. The triumphs of liberalism hit the top of a cycle just before the

*Reform by statute became a primary characteristic of
American law as the frontier rapidly expanded. The passage
of the homestead acts during this period made the
acquisition of land progressively easier for the settler.*

Civil War, when a public school system was established.

The widespread use of the law as a police power did not
appear until later, but there was a prelude to this development
well before the Civil War in the form of elaborate constitutional provisions respecting banks, railroads, and canals and
in statutes requiring periodical or cash payments of wages.
Income taxes in the modern sense were adopted in the 1830s
and 1840s in six states. The entire period was marked by
vigorous social consciousness—great moral movements in
the political arena (for example, Prohibition and women's
rights)—and an altruistic effort on a vast scale for the poor.
Two hallmarks of the time were the homestead laws and the
abolition of imprisonment for debt.

During this period women achieved the first real (if primitive) recognition of their legal rights. A narrow protection in
property rights accorded married women by equity was
widened by statutes that placed them on a rough equality
with their husbands. Judicial liberalism supplemented this
legislation, although in a haphazard and limited fashion, with
the recognition of a wife's right to compensation for the loss
of the society of her consort. Such developments grew out of
women's equal participation in the hazards and hardships of
frontier life. Children also received some protection against

parental cruelty; parents were held responsible for any crimes they committed against children. Reformatories were established for delinquent youths, but the criminal liability of minors was little altered. The notion of a juvenile court system did not appear until the turn of the century.

In the laws of property the complex old regime was streamlined somewhat. The rules of inheritance were greatly changed in favor of parents, surviving spouses, and half-blood and, to a lesser extent, illegitimate children. Heirs and next-of-kin became generally identical under the law. Estates, however they were acquired from the paternal or the maternal side, were made to descend in the same manner. All real estate became included in execution and administration assets, making it liable for payment of debts, with few preferences.

Despite these highly significant changes and the emergence of a system that would be readily recognizable to a mid-twentieth-century lawyer, legislative reform in the area during this period was always partial, casual, and unsatisfactory. There were innumerable variations from state to state. Fundamental distinctions between real property and personal property continued to be made, as did distinctions between legal and equitable interests. In short, the state of property law during the period can only be described as erratic.

The law of equity, on the other hand, developed with relative consistency. This is not to say that its development was greeted with wild enthusiasm. From its English beginnings, equity had been a gloss on the common law. It was a subsidiary, but historically separate, system for dispensing justice for the particular purpose at hand, according to numerous general principles. It was restricted to cases for which the common law provided an inadequate remedy. Because of its clearly subjective nature, however, equity was a system of dubious value to the early Americans, who wanted clear-cut guidelines. Partly for this reason, equity spread slowly and in a piecemeal fashion. It was dependent largely on statutory grant, particularly in Massachusetts and Pennsylvania.

The infiltration of equity into law in such states was a unique detail of the American legal experiment. No American court ever exercised the wholesale powers of the English courts of chancery. Unlike the British version, equity in America was never really a separate system as much as a supplemental notion to a unitary system. This American system of one court with jurisdiction over matters of both law and equity was ensured under the codes of civil procedure that were adopted in many states from 1848 on. These codes, which provided for the administrative fusion of law and equity, was the high point of a movement to reduce rules and doctrines to a settled body of law.

A corollary goal was to streamline the judicial process so that both legal and equitable rights could be determined in one civil case. The leader of the codification movement was a New York lawyer, David Dudley Field (1805–94). He never achieved complete popular or theoretical success, but the Field codes for New York and California, which he authored, provided the model for the later Federal Rules for Civil Procedure. Adopted in 1938, these rules established on the federal level what the states had done a hundred years before.

Under the rules the federal courts received the same types of dual powers that the state courts had enjoyed since the previous century. These rules, in their complete fusion of law and equity and in their simplification of practice and procedure, were a major achievement in law reform and served as a model for the states. Ironically, the result did not weaken equitable principles but gave them new vigor and applicability.

In some ways, popular control and influence in this period debased the state judiciaries. Examples of this phenomenon were the restriction of the power of trial judges and the popular selection of judges generally. Restriction of power was simple but overwhelmingly significant: the American trial judge was limited to a bare restatement of the evidence in his charge to the jury, whereas the English trial judge had the power to weigh and comment in detail on the evidence and its significance. The roots of this fundamental change lay in the trend to popular selection of judges. Until 1798, all nonfederal judges were appointed by the governors or elected by the legislatures. By 1840 popular election was characteristic, and thereafter it increased steadily.

There was also a tendency to shorten the term of tenure, a practice that arose naturally from the democratic fear that power tends to grow less responsible when it is exercised for long periods by the same person. Such distrust was fueled by the power of almost any judge to declare legislation unconstitutional and to issue injunctions. Elective terms of judges, however, have always been long, as compared with those of other public officials. The twentieth century has proved that it is possible for the elective process to attract and retain competent judges. There has been a growing tendency in the last generation to seek so-called merit selection of judges; this involves gubernatorial appointment of judges from lists of applicants deemed qualified by bipartisan committees composed of both lawyers and nonlawyers. In most states, however, direct election of judges is still the usual method of selection.

The bench, popularly elected, was both liberal and able; in some states, notably the South, it was brilliant. The legislatures were generally characterized by rationalism and a high degree of enlightenment. The bar dominated the legislatures and enjoyed a social and political prestige that was to diminish markedly in later years. On the whole the period was one of contradictions but also one of substantial accomplishment.

After 1868

The Fourteenth Amendment to the Constitution, which became effective in 1868, prohibited the states from depriving any person "of life, liberty, or property without due process of law" or denying any person "the equal protection of the law." It profoundly altered the relation between state and federal courts and distinctly marked the beginning of a new period in the legal development of the country. Attempts to define the term *due process* and to delimit the extent of the states' police power made the federal courts the background for testing the social legislation that stemmed from the complex economic and industrial conditions after the Civil War.

Many important cases involving corporations also came before the same courts, for corporations are "persons" under the Fourteenth Amendment and "citizens" for purposes of federal jurisdiction. Moreover, since corporations carry on most of the business and own a large percentage of all the property in the United States (Justice Stephen Field of the U.S. Supreme Court estimated it at eighty percent in 1890), the matter continues to have immense social significance.

The enlarged freedoms of nineteenth-century democracy did not greatly affect the treatment of industrial property. Yale University President Arthur Twining Hadley observed: "For at least sixty years after the adoption of universal (male) suffrage the tendency was all in the other direction—to legislate *for* the property owner rather than against him; to strengthen the powers of capital rather than diminish them. ... The small protection given to the rights of man, as compared with that which was accorded to the rights of property, is a salient feature in the early history of every American state—and sometimes of its later history also."

The reason for this undoubtedly lay in the loose economic framework of society. Cheap land created a group of free-holders without class distinctions: anyone who aimed high might rise high. Radicalism in such a society could gain little headway. It came instead with the development of great urban centers and a more industrialized economy. The rural population was ninety percent of the total in 1800, a little less by 1850, but less than half by the census of 1920.

Industrial regulation, as we have come to know it today, began about 1870 with the regulation of the railroads. Its development "shook the foundation of state and national politics for a generation." There was a subsequent increase in administrative commissions with investigative powers subject to limited judicial review. There is an American tendency to standardize procedure and in the United States—much more so than in England—a great field of administrative law is developing. Trade regulation began to increase rapidly in the United States only in the late nineteenth century; for example, pure-food laws, later to become universal, began in 1892.

The legal status of the American industrial worker is unique. On the one hand, the Thirteenth Amendment to the Constitution, which prohibits "involuntary servitude," prevents a worker from being forced to work, or fulfill a contract, against his will. On the other hand, this immunity was relatively worthless as long as the worker was unprotected against unfair agreements that were entered into because of his economic needs. The tendency in the late nineteenth and early twentieth centuries was to uphold long-hour, low-pay contracts as functions of "freedom of contract" on the part of employer and worker. Union shops were blocked by so-called right-to-work laws. Even as late as the 1920s the U.S. Supreme Court struck down as unconstitutional laws that limited the number of hours that men and children could be forced to work under contract. One case prompted Oliver Wendell Holmes (a Supreme Court justice, 1902–32) to complain bitterly in dissent that "the Fourteenth Amendment did not enact Mr. Herbert Spencer's Social Statics." Not until the 1930s was this trend reversed. It did not take as long for workers to gain the protection of workmen's compensation laws (first enacted in 1902), but the resistence to them was equally firm.

Judges in the late nineteenth century devised a number of

doctrines—among which the classic was "contributory negligence"—in order to prevent employees from being compensated for injuries they suffered on the job. After 1910, however, all the states adopted workmen's compensation acts entitling the injured worker to compensation without reference to common-law notions of fault.

The range of social legislation widened immensely. Much of it was purely moralistic (against gambling, racing, cigarettes, liquor, sexual activities, and so forth). The treatment of women, however, merits special attention. The twentieth century saw the demise of the old common-law fiction that the bride's legal personality merged into that of her husband upon marriage. Within the family the married woman began to attain substantial equality with her husband in the realm of property and domestic relations. In industry the attempt to give women special protection was a storm center of agitation. In both areas, the attitude toward women was markedly paternalistic (for example, in purchases of property and credit practices).

Divorce laws were enacted in all states, with causes running from adultery to a score or more of others, including mental cruelty and incompatibility. Such causes in many instances became covers for mutual consent, although it was not until well after World War II that so-called no-fault divorce legislation replaced the unpleasant adversary method developed in the late nineteenth century. Informal common-law marriage still exists in many states, and, as more and more unmarried couples live together, courts have had to work out property settlements for the unmarried in much the same way as for the married.

2.
The Impulse to Codify

The history of American law is, in a sense, the story of flirtations with codification (adopting codes of civil procedure). The process of codifying the law, after the flurry of activity that began before the Civil War, temporarily ceased but began again in a new form during the first half of the twentieth century. Five codes of penal and of substantive civil law, thirty codes of civil procedure, and about thirty codes of criminal procedure were mainly the products of the earlier movement.

The National Conference of Commissioners on Uniform State Laws had prepared more than one hundred uniform acts of law by the late 1970s. Of these, a half-dozen in the commercial field were the most successful, being adopted in from half to all jurisdictions. The American Law Institute, in which teachers of law predominate, has prepared restatements of various branches of the law and model codes in criminal law, criminal procedure, and other areas, all designed to promote uniformity of essential principles. Although seldom enacted as a whole, the model codes have profoundly influenced both courts and legislatures. Other major sources of expertise for state legislatures are legislative drafting bureaus, which first began in 1890 and now exist in practically every state.

Inconsistent Principles

The impulse to codify the law was a response to the uncertainty in the law—in the nineteenth century due largely to a void and in the mid-twentieth century to the unwieldy bulk of judicial law. Since the early 1880s, the West Publishing Co. of St. Paul, Minn., has published case law reports for every region of the country and for the entire federal system. Well-indexed and thorough, the reports were a beacon for the judge and practitioner who needed to know "what the law is."

Today, however, the sheer volume of case law makes the law uncertain even if accessible. The number of annual volumes of American reports is in the thousands. The cases cited by the courts in any volume run into hundreds and frequently into thousands, from many jurisdictions. Multitudes of cases from varieties of jurisdictions produce inconsistent principles and paradoxical results. The law in sophisticated fields is not only beyond the power of any lay person to discover or comprehend but it is also frequently unavailable even to those with access to standard libraries.

The Process of Interpretation

In a sense, codification has always been an illusion. To hope for certainty from a written code is to ignore or grossly underestimate the difficult and necessary function of applying that code and interpreting its meaning in situations where its terms do not provide a clear-cut answer to the question in dispute. "General propositions," Justice Oliver Wendell Holmes wrote, "do not decide concrete cases." It is the process of interpretation that gives the law its texture, shape, and definition. And this process is no less susceptible to the frailties of the actors than is any other process in human institutions. The common law, however, from Blackstone on, has always claimed for itself more certainty and more mystery than it really ever could have.

A great deal has wisely been said on the necessity of providing guidance for legislation and judicial decision by use of a functional test of social utility; however, no efficient way of objectively assessing the relative efficacy of substantive legal rules has ever been developed. Legislative bureaus in the substantive area and judicial councils in the procedural field (both creatures of the early twentieth century) were expected to do just this, but neither was able to fill the bill adequately. What did happen was that the revolt created by the labor struggle spread to social workers, social scientists, the law schools, and even to the bar. It opened a new epoch in the law of the country. A similar development occurred in the past generation with the struggle for racial equality in both law and fact. The final outcome of the struggle, despite massive changes, is not yet clear, but its shape is not too dissimilar institutionally from that of the earlier period.

II. Federal Law in America

"The good of the people is the highest law."

—Cicero

3.
The Constitution and the Federal System

The public law of the United States revolves largely around the federal system, the written Constitution, and the judicial construction of written constitutions. These three elements are closely related because the U.S. Supreme Court has from an early time been the final authority that determines the respective powers of the United States and of the states under the written Constitution of the country; and each state supreme court, within its own territory, is the final arbiter of state governmental power under that state's written constitution.

The Federal System

Plans for colonial federation were proposed several times even before the end of the American Revolution. The movement of the colonies against Great Britain that finally led to independence forced some degree of unity, and the First Continental Congress, which assembled in Philadelphia in 1774, was the outward symbol of unity of political action. What little political direction there was came through the continuance of this kind of organization, but there was no formal written instrument of union. So arranged, the system was highly insufficient. It was replaced by the Articles of Confederation in 1781.

The Articles of Confederation established a loose union of states, with little in the way of a national government. The government had no power, for example, to raise revenue or to enforce its orders by action directed immediately toward the citizens of the United States. The confederation had the authority to ask the state to act but not to compel action either by the state or by its citizens. It could make treaties but had no power to enforce state observance of such treaties. Each state had power to impose restrictions upon trade with other states. A state with the geographical advantages of New York was in a position to impose—and did impose—burdensome restrictions upon the commerce of its neighbors—New Jersey and Connecticut.

Prior to the adoption of the Constitution, the geographical advantages of New York Harbor made it possible for the state to impose restrictions upon the commerce of its neighbors. The power conferred upon the federal government by the Constitution to control interstate commerce alleviated the situation.

Such conditions could not continue for long. They led to the assembling of the federal convention of 1787 and to the framing and adoption of the Constitution of the United States, under which the government was established in 1789. The Constitution was framed with specific reference to the difficulties that had existed before its adoption. A governmental organization was set up independent of that in the states and with power to enforce its commands directly upon the citizens of the states. Broad powers were expressly cor- · ferred, the most important of which were the powers to control interstate and foreign commerce, to levy taxes and raise federal revenues independently of the states, and to control foreign relations. Thus a central government with real authority was constituted.

The history of the federal system since 1789 is largely a history of the expansion of the importance and authority of the national government under this Constitution. This expansion has been accomplished in several ways: by a broadened construction of the original provisions of the Constitution of 1787; by amendment of the Constitution; by the development of means of transportation and communication, which increased enormously the number of transactions in interstate and foreign commerce subject to national control; and by the increased number of states, most of which were created out of territory belonging to the national government.

The Written Constitution

The written Constitution is an essential element of the federal system in the United States, for there must be some authoritative statement of the respective powers of both country and states. The written constitution is not essential to state government in the United States, but each state has from its beginning had such a constitution.

The U.S. Constitution is a relatively brief document, as are a few of the earlier state constitutions. The typical state constitution, however, came to be a lengthy document that not only organized and imposed limitations upon the state government but also contained a great mass of detailed legislation. This legislative detail is frequently altered by state constitutional amendments. In theory the national government has only such powers as are granted to it by the national Constitution, whereas a state government has all powers not denied it by the national Constitution and the constitution of the state. This might naturally suggest that national powers are strictly construed and state legislative authority is broadly construed, but because of the long and detailed state constitutions, the opposite has become true. Under broad constitutional grants of national authority, the U.S. Supreme Court has, from the first, tended to be liberal in the construction of national power. Under the detailed state constitutions, which do some hedging about the powers of state legislatures, state courts have tended toward a narrow construction of such powers.

The Judicial Construction

Some device is necessary in a federal system to preserve the barriers between federal and state powers. The U.S. Supreme Court serves as this agent. More controversially, it also serves as the final authority in other cases for determining the powers of Congress and the executive department under the federal Constitution. (State supreme courts perform similar functions with respect to powers under state constitutions.) The courts of both country and states refuse to pass upon certain questions that they term political, but apart from this they regularly decide issues arising under their written constitutions. The power of the courts to determine the constitutionality of legislation, first asserted in New Jersey in 1780, has been generally recognized since the decision of the U.S. Supreme Court in *Marbury* v. *Madison* (1803).

The more detailed the constitutions and the greater the

tendency to exercise governmental power to solve new indus- trial and social needs, the more often are the courts called upon to construe written constitutions. Because numerous restrictions have been imposed on legislative action by consti- tutional texts, practically every important federal and state law comes to the courts to have its validity determined—at least in part if not in whole. This gives to judicial decisions a proportionately greater emphasis than they really deserve: the final determination of constitutionality—and thus validi- ty—is made by a court, which, by definition, must make its decision on the technical issues of constitutional construction and not on the actual merits of the legislation. The line is difficult to draw in some cases, of course, and depends to some extent on each justice's conception of the task at hand. Problems of constitutional construction have become more important and more difficult in the fields of administrative law and in the administration of criminal justice.

The importance of administrative law was recognized in the 1930s when administrative agencies were established to cope with new economic and social problems. Congress dele- gated wide authority to permanent federal and state boards. But both national and state constitutions organize govern- ments into three departments (legislative, executive, and judi- cial) and forbid by implication the delegation of lawmaking authority. The courts must decide what the authorized func- tions of each department are and which legislative powers may not be delegated. Pressures of practical necessity have forced the courts to uphold wide delegations of rule-making power to administrative agencies and authorizations for agencies to make what appear to be judicial determinations (such as imposition of fines and penalties). These results have been the product of the construction of broad constitutional provisions, and—although wise—the logic employed to dis- tinguish later cases from earlier ones has often been amusing.

The federal courts, especially the Supreme Court, did not immediately uphold the constitutionality of such delegations of power. Indeed, the early and mid-1930s witnessed decision after decision striking down federal statutes and administra- tive programs as "unconstitutional." Not until 1937 did the Supreme Court, under both internal and external pressure, begin to construe the powers of Congress more broadly. Af- ter 1937, decisions by the Supreme Court invalidating acts of Congress became extremely rare, and decisions invalidating state economic regulation only slightly less so.

The change in attitude was no mere yielding to expediency, nor was it an abdication of the judicial function. It reflected the Court's acceptance of a principle of self-restraint, long advocated by dissenting justices such as Benjamin N. Cardozo, Harlan Fiske Stone, and Louis D. Brandeis. The Court realized that it needed to embrace a philosophy of constitutional construction that would not paralyze the government as it attempted to deal with changing social conditions; there was increased tolerance for change and for economic policy that might be distasteful to the justices. Above all, there was a new deference to the constitutional function of the legislative branch—a willingness to recognize that the courts are not the only guardians of the Constitution and, moreover, that they are not the agency best equipped to determine the most appropriate means to proper governmental ends. Implicit in this attitude was the belief that the political process must be the first line of defense against legislative error or excess.

The function of the Supreme Court in constitutional cases nevertheless remains enormously important, especially in cases where political restraints are inadequate, such as where the impact of state or federal legislation impinges on the interests of minority groups. The French writer Alexis de Tocqueville noted that "the power vested in the American courts of justice of pronouncing a statute to be unconstitutional forms one of the most powerful barriers that have ever been devised against the tyranny of political assemblies."

The Supreme Court is not the only court with power to declare statutes or practices unconstitutional under the federal Constitution, of course. The federal district courts and the eleven federal courts of appeal, along with state courts, all enjoy the same power. Indeed, the tendency of the Supreme Court in recent years has been to encourage state courts to bear a much heavier burden in providing constitutional protection to citizens.

4.
The Supreme Court of the United States

The Supreme Court of the United States is the ultimate tribunal in a dual system of courts—state and federal. The court is also the final interpreter of the meaning of the U.S. Constitution.

Within the framework of litigation, the Court marks the boundaries of authority between state and nation, state and state, and government and citizen. As the third, or judicial, branch of government, it is equal to, yet in theory independent of, the executive and legislative branches.

Creation and Membership

The Articles of Confederation, which loosely governed the country from 1781 until the adoption of the Constitution, did not provide for a national court, although Congress was permitted to appoint courts of appeal in cases of naval captures. Until 1787 such a court operated, deciding more than a hundred appeals from state courts. The framers of the Constitution, however, recognized the need for a national court with stature equal, in theory, to that of the Congress and the executive branch. Article III, Section 1, of the Constitution makes these provisions:

> *The judicial Power of the United States, shall be vested in one supreme Court, and in such inferior Courts as the Congress may from time to time ordain and establish. The Judges, both of the superior and inferior Courts, shall hold their Offices during good Behavior, and shall, at stated Times, receive for their Services, a Compensation, which shall not be diminished during their Continuance in Office.*

Section 2 further defines the scope of power, or jurisdiction, of the federal court:

> *The judicial Power shall extend to all Cases, in Law and Equity, arising under this Constitution, the Laws of the United States, and Treaties made, or which shall be*

A contemporary cartoon titled "Nine Old Men" depicts the Supreme Court in 1937. President Franklin D. Roosevelt attempted to increase the size of the Court during the same year to obtain majority support for his New Deal programs.

made, under their Authority;—to all Cases affecting Ambassadors, other public Ministers and Consuls;—to all cases of Admiralty and maritime Jurisdiction;—to Controversies to which the United States shall be a Party;—to Controversies between two or more States;— between a State and Citizens of another State;—between Citizens of different States,—between Citizens of the

same State claiming Lands under Grants of different States, and between a State, or the Citizens thereof, and foreign States, Citizens or Subjects.

By implication, state and local courts are left with the task of hearing disputes involving only local interests. The role of the lower federal courts, from the time they were established by the Judicial Act of 1789, has thus been highly specialized. The exact details of the specialization were left by the Constitution to Congress. In exercising its duties under Article III to "ordain and establish" lower federal courts, Congress could even abolish them if it pleased. Of these courts, only the Supreme Court is given by Article III a status independent of the will of Congress.

The Supreme Court is not entirely free from congressional action, however. The Constitution does not specify the size of the Court or the exact sweep of its appellate jurisdiction. The Court originally was composed of a chief justice and five associate judges. Membership was increased successively to seven (1807), nine (1837), and ten (1863). In 1866, as part of the effort by Congress to curb the appointing power of President Andrew Johnson, a statute cut the size of the Court to seven, as vacancies should occur. (The Court actually shrank only to eight members.) Membership was increased in 1869 to nine, where it has since remained. President Franklin D. Roosevelt tried to increase the size of the Court in 1937 in order to obtain a majority sympathetic to the constitutionality of his New Deal programs. Although Roosevelt's attempt failed, the public furor over "court packing" served as a reminder that congressional control over the size and jurisdiction of the Court was of more than historical significance.

Congress has a more indirect, but no less important, effect on the Court: the appointment process. Appointments to the Supreme Court, as to all federal courts, are made by the president, subject to approval by the Senate. Eleven nominations to the Supreme Court have been rejected by the Senate, the most recent in 1969 and in 1970. The Constitution does not list qualifications for office; however, all appointees have been lawyers, although only a minority have had prior experience as judges. Geographic distribution has been a factor, but the primary consideration has most often been the political outlook of the nominee—not his party but his view of the Court's role in the body politic. The consideration is easier to state than to apply: a number of justices have surprised and disappointed the presidents who appointed them. The most conspicuous examples of this phenomenon were Justice Oliver Wendell Holmes, whose apparent "pro-business" opinions were a bitter disappointment to President Theodore Roosevelt, and Chief Justice Earl Warren, whose appointment President Dwight D. Eisenhower later called "my biggest mistake."

The tenure of a Supreme Court appointment under Article III of the Constitution is "good behavior." A justice may be removed from office only if impeached and convicted by the Senate (Article II, Section 4, of the Constitution). Only one

President Jimmy Carter (front row, center) meets with the Supreme Court justices in the White House Rose Garden. The nine justices include (from left to right, top to bottom) Harry Blackmun, Potter Stewart, William Rehnquist, Chief Justice Warren Burger, Thurgood Marshall, Lewis Powell, William Brennan, Byron White, and John Paul Stevens.

justice has ever been impeached—Samuel Chase, who was acquitted in 1805. Only one justice, Abe Fortas, has ever resigned under pressure. He left the bench in 1969 after extensive publicity about his outside financial activities.

The longest tenure, of more than thirty-six years, was that of William O. Douglas. Two chief justices, Edward D. White and Harlan F. Stone, were advanced to that office while associate justices. Charles Evans Hughes, who was chief justice from 1930 to 1941, had served as associate justice before resigning in 1916 to run for president.

Basic Functions

The principal duty of the Supreme Court is to reconsider important questions of federal and constitutional law that have been first decided in a lower federal or state court, but wrongly, in the view of one of the litigants. In doing so, the Court has from an early date exercised the power to declare acts of Congress and of state legislatures to be unconstitutional (the power of "judicial review"). This power is not mentioned, let alone defined, in the Constitution, and it was not established without intense partisan and sectional resentment.

Judicial review of acts of Congress was established in 1803

Justices of the United

Chief Justices

John Jay	1789-1795
John Rutledge	1795
Oliver Ellsworth	1796-1800
John Marshall	1801-1835
Roger B. Taney	1836-1864
Salmon P. Chase	1864-1873
Morrison R. Waite	1874-1888
Melville W. Fuller	1888-1910
Edward D. White	1910-1921
William H. Taft	1921-1930
Charles E. Hughes	1930-1941
Harlan F. Stone	1941-1946
Fred M. Vinson	1946-1953
Earl Warren	1953-1969
Warren E. Burger	1969

Associate Justices

John Rutledge	1789-1791
William Cushing	1789-1810
James Wilson	1789-1798
John Blair	1789-1796
James Iredell	1790-1799
Thomas Johnson	1792-1793
William Paterson	1793-1806
Samuel Chase	1796-1811
Bushrod Washington	1798-1829
Alfred Moore	1800-1804
William Johnson	1804-1834
Henry Brockholst Livingston	1806-1823
Thomas Todd	1807-1826
Joseph Story	1811-1845
Gabriel Duval	1812-1835
Smith Thompson	1823-1843
Robert Trimble	1826-1828
John McLean	1829-1861
Henry Baldwin	1830-1844
James M. Wayne	1835-1867
Philip P. Barbour	1836-1841
John Catron	1837-1865
John McKinley	1837-1852
Peter V. Daniel	1841-1860
Samuel Nelson	1845-1872
Levi Woodbury	1845-1851
Robert C. Grier	1846-1870
Benjamin Curtis	1851-1857
John A. Campbell	1853-1861
Nathan Clifford	1858-1881
Noah H. Swayne	1862-1881
Samuel F. Miller	1862-1890
David Davis	1862-1877
Stephen J. Field	1863-1897
William Strong	1870-1880
Joseph P. Bradley	1870-1892
Ward Hunt	1872-1882
John M. Harlan	1877-1911
William B. Woods	1880-1887

States Supreme Court

Stanley Matthews	1881-1889	Owen J. Roberts	1930-1945
Horace Gray	1881-1902	Benjamin N.	
Samuel		Cardozo	1932-1938
Blatchford	1882-1893	Hugo L. Black	1937-1971
Lucius Q. C.		Stanley Reed	1938-1957
Lamar	1888-1893	Felix Frankfurter	1939-1962
David J. Brewer	1889-1910	William O.	
Henry B. Brown	1890-1906	Douglas	1939-1976
George Shiras	1892-1903	Frank Murphy	1940-1949
Howell E. Jackson	1893-1895	James F. Byrnes	1941-1942
Edward D. White	1894-1910	Robert H. Jackson	1941-1954
Rufus W. Peckham	1895-1909	Wiley B. Rutledge	1943-1949
Joseph McKenna	1898-1925	Harold H. Burton	1945-1958
Oliver W. Holmes	1902-1932	Thomas C. Clark	1949-1967
William R. Day	1903-1922	Sherman Minton	1949-1956
William H. Moody	1906-1910	John M. Harlan	1955-1971
Horace H. Lurton	1910-1914	William J.	
Charles E. Hughes	1910-1916	Brennan, Jr.	1956-
Willis		Charles E.	
Van Devanter	1910-1937	Whittaker	1957-1962
Joseph R. Lamar	1911-1916	Potter Stewart	1958-
Mahlon Pitney	1912-1922	Byron R. White	1962-
James C.		Arthur J. Goldberg	1962-1965
McReynolds	1914-1941	Abe Fortas	1965-1969
Louis D. Brandeis	1916-1939	Thurgood	
John H. Clarke	1916-1922	Marshall	1967-
George		Harry A.	
Sutherland	1922-1938	Blackmun	1970-
Pierce Butler	1922-1939	Lewis F. Powell, Jr.	1972-
Edward T.		William H.	
Sanford	1923-1930	Rehnquist	1972-
Harlan F. Stone	1925-1941	John Paul Stevens	1975-

in the celebrated case of *Marbury* v. *Madison*, although it had been assumed to be proper in an earlier case. The opinion of Chief Justice John Marshall, which adopted in substance the argument of Alexander Hamilton in No. 78 of *The Federalist* papers (a series of 85 essays in defense of the Constitution), was based on logical deduction and not on case law. It stated that if the decision of a case involves a conflict between a statute and the Constitution, the Supreme Court—which is bound to render decisions according to "law"—must prefer the higher law (the Constitution) to the inferior (the statute). Marshall's decision has been criticized on two levels—first, for begging the question (who—the Court, the Congress, or the electorate—decides when there is a conflict?); and, second, for usurping power not intended for the Court. Although Marshall's opinion is not logically flawless, it is consistent with earlier state court practices and with oblique references in the Constitutional Convention to the doctrine of judicial review.

The importance of the doctrine in the Marbury case was hidden somewhat by the actual consequence of the decision: by holding an act of Congress to be unconstitutional, the Court found itself with no jurisdiction over the matter and was thus unable to touch the defendant, President Thomas Jefferson's secretary of state. The Court, speaking through Chief Justice Marshall, thus avoided a head-on clash with the Anti-Federalists. The irony of this act of Court abstention tended to blunt the popular awareness, for the moment at least, of the Court's assertion of power.

When the Court asserted the power thirteen years later to declare unconstitutional the acts of state legislatures, the reaction was not nearly as muted. A number of attempts were made in Congress, all unsuccessful, to strip the Court of jurisdiction over constitutional questions arising from state courts. Originally centered in the South, resistance spread to the North several years later in the period just before the Civil War. The doctrine did not cease to be controversial until after the war.

Judicial review of legislation is not the only tool the Court brings to its task of umpiring the federal system. Executive, administrative, and judicial actions also are subject to review by the Supreme Court. The effect of these and other similar activities is to both pacify and unify. By hearing boundary disputes between states or controversies over water rights to interstate rivers, for example, the Court serves as a substitute for the tensions of diplomacy or conflict. And by providing a national interpretation of federal laws, the Court eliminates the divergency of viewpoints toward these laws that might otherwise rise in the lower courts.

Jurisdiction and Procedure

The Court seldom serves as a court of *first* resort. Very few cases are brought in the "original jurisdiction" of the court, except for controversies between states, between a state and the United States, or between ambassadors. Most of the Court's business comes from lower federal and state courts. Depending on the nature of the decision in the lower court, the route to the Supreme Court is by either appeal or certiorari ("to be informed"). The Court is obliged to decide appeals but need not decide cases on certiorari. If the Court declines a case on certiorari, the decision of the lower court is automatically sustained.

The development of this "two-headed jurisdiction" reflects a response by Congress to a long struggle by the Court to cope with an ever-increasing workload. The problem is an old one, which Congress first addressed in 1891 by creating the Circuit Court of Appeals Act, setting up courts to hear appeals from federal district (trial) courts. The circuit courts were given final authority over all appeals except for cases of exceptional public importance. The Judiciary Act of 1925 carried reforms further. Sponsored by the Court itself, under the aegis of Chief Justice William Howard Taft, the act greatly limited the number of cases the Court was required to decide by placing the vast majority of cases under its discretionary, certiorari jurisdiction. The Court was left with a small percentage of cases in its obligatory appeal jurisdiction. The overall effect was to give the Court broad control over the cases it would decide.

Each justice considers each of the more than four thousand cases that come to the Court in a year. Less than five percent of these cases receive full treatment by the Court (written briefs, approximately one hour of oral argument, and written opinion); the Court simply refuses to hear the other cases.

Decisions on requests to hear cases (largely petitions for certiorari) and on cases that have been argued are made weekly during the Court's term (October through June) at a conference of the justices. The responsibility of writing the opinion for the Court in an argued case is assigned after these conferences by the chief justice (or by the senior associate justice if the chief justice is in the minority). The practice of writing dissenting opinions is as old as the Marshall Court (1801–35); the first resolute dissenter was Marshall's colleague William Johnson. In the event a majority opinion cannot be obtained, the Court may rehear the case, but a tie involving a reversal of a lower court upholds that court.

"It's nothing personal, Prescott. It's just that a higher court gets a kick out of overruling a lower court."

Changing Roles and Effects

Any assessment of the unifying forces in American life must credit the Supreme Court with playing an important role. Judicial review of state legislation takes its place as a force along with physical factors, such as transportation and communication, and political factors, such as political parties and presidential leadership. Two parts of the Constitution, the commerce clause (Art. I, Sect. 8) and the equal protection clause (Section 1 of the Fourteenth Amendment), have been the chief technical instruments used by the Court in this context.

The commerce clause granted Congress the power to "regulate commerce among the several states." With only this sparse constitutional command, the Court has, from the time of Marshall, nullified state tax laws and regulations that discriminate against or unduly burden interstate commerce. The common, national commerce market has thereby been maintained and encouraged against the demands of local protectionism. Thus, in successive periods the Court has attempted to weigh state laws in light of local needs against the inroad on the common, national market. Marshall's Court tended to stress the national imperative. In the Court of Chief Justice Roger Brooke Taney (1836–64) the concern was for local need. These competing themes have reappeared at different times.

The assertion of a national interest over commerce, established by the Marshall Court in the early nineteenth century, laid the groundwork for congressional legislation late in the century. Beginning with the Interstate Commerce Act of 1887 and the Sherman Anti-Trust Act of 1890, Congress gradually took over regulation of parts of the economy that the states previously had policed ineffectively or not at all, held back as they were by judicial limitations or practical inhibitions.

Early in this century, a series of decisions, of which the child labor case in 1918 was primary, threatened to create a no-man's-land, where neither federal nor state government could constitutionally control commerce effectively. Not until the overruling of the child labor case in 1941 was the federal power over commerce placed on a firm basis. Subsequently the Court sustained far-reaching applications of the commerce power by Congress. The most striking example was a decision approving the limiting of wheat production, which included the wheat consumed on the farm where it was grown. Very recently, however, the Court has begun to cut back on the power of Congress over commerce. In 1976 the Court held that the commerce power must yield to state and municipal rights in the area of minimum-wage laws.

What the commerce clause has been to national control of the economy, the due process and equal protection clauses of the Fourteenth Amendment have been to citizens and corporations seeking protection from arbitrary and repressive acts by the government. The Fourteenth Amendment, enacted after the Civil War, guarantees that no state shall "... deprive any person of life, liberty, or property, without due process of law...." The Court soon interpreted the clause to mean that it protected against the substance of legislation as well as against arbitrary procedures set up by legislation. But the earliest common use of "substantive due process," as it came to be called, was to invalidate social legislation—such as minimum-wage/maximum-hour laws. The Court's dominant majority accepted a laissez-faire economic philosophy—one that favored minimum governmental interference in economic affairs. In its decision the Court claimed to be upholding "freedom of contract." The decisions paralyzed experimental social legislation and drew a current of powerful dissents by justices Oliver Wendell Holmes and Louis D. Brandeis. Beginning about 1940, after both Holmes and Brandeis had left the Court, the doctrines embodied in their dissents became the law of the land.

Civil liberties in the United States have had a markedly different and much shorter history. It was not until the 1920s that the protection of the First Amendment—the freedoms of speech, the press, assembly, and religion—was also applied by the Court to the states as part of the liberty guaranteed by the Fourteenth Amendment. As the Court has become more tolerant of economic controls, it has taken a stricter view of laws that curtail the First Amendment liberties and the procedural safeguards of the Bill of Rights.

The other important clause of the Fourteenth Amendment guarantees that no state shall "... deny to any person ... the equal protection of the laws." The clause has had a development similar to the evolution of due process of law. Originally designed for the benefit of the emancipated Negroes, soon used as a shield against progressive social legislation, it came to serve as a barrier to racially discriminatory laws.

In a steady series of cases the Court invalidated a variety of restrictions directed at Negroes: exclusion from voting in party primary elections, racial zoning, enforcement of racially restrictive convenants in real estate deeds, exclusion from state-maintained universities, and enforced segregation in public schools and on public conveyances.

Race is not the only status that has been sheltered under the equal protection clause against discriminatory legislative classifications. An expanded guarantee of "equal protection" has been extended to aliens, illegitimate children, the indigent, and women. The Court has proceeded more equivocally in these areas, however, and has upheld some statutory schemes that it most likely would have struck down had the classification been racial. Part of the reason may be that the Court, especially during the last several years, has become increasingly sensitive to the question of whether the extension of such protection should be a function of the judiciary or of Congress (under its power to enforce the Fourteenth Amendment) and state legislatures.

It is no surprise that the Court, exercising power of such gravity, delicacy, and finality, has frequently found itself un-

der attack—both popular and partisan. Given the generality of the language in the Constitution and the duty to apply such language to an evolving social, economic, and political order, the Court cannot escape rendering judgments that displease many.

A number of the strongest presidents have pitted themselves against the Court at one time or another. Thomas Jefferson and Andrew Jackson found a number of Marshall's opinions decidedly distasteful. Abraham Lincoln called for reexamination of the Dred Scott decision but stopped short of counseling open resistance to it. Theodore Roosevelt, irked by judicial decisions that invalidated social legislation, asked unsuccessfully for popular recall of judges and popular referenda on court decisions.

Franklin D. Roosevelt went so far in 1937 as to propose that the size of the Supreme Court be enlarged to as many as fifteen justices in order to eliminate the Court majority that steadfastly had opposed his national recovery program on constitutional grounds. His plan, defeated by Congress, had provided for the appointment of one justice for each sitting justice who had been on the court ten years and was seventy years old. Meanwhile, the Court had given clear signs in intervening decisions that it would be more sympathetic in defining the scope of governmental power under the Constitution.

Self-limitation

From its earliest days the Supreme Court has recognized that its decisions are capable of provoking the most profound controversy. In order to maintain its legitimacy and to keep controversy to a minimum, the Court has developed doctrines of self-limitation. It will not give "advisory opinions" to other branches of the government on the constitutionality of proposed actions or decide a case on constitutional grounds if a nonconstitutional ground is available. Nor will it render a constitutional decision broader than that required by the facts of the case before it. Within the past generation the Court has developed a "political question" doctrine that leaves issues for resolution by other branches of government.

These canons of self-limitation, like other doctrines, are not rigid or immune from change. A Court interested in effecting social change is unlikely to emphasize either technical prerequisites to decision making or self-imposed limitations on those decisions. A Court that views social change as the function of other branches of government is likely to insist on both.

Important Decisions and Trends

The Marshall Court laid the basis for a federal union capable of effective government. Under Marshall, congressional powers were construed expansively and the Supreme Court's position was firmly established. Marshall's successor as chief justice, Roger Brooke Taney, guided a court more sympathetic to concerns of the states. The Taney Court, however, did not reverse the current. Taney's reputation turns, justly or unjustly, on the Dred Scott case, *Scott* v. *Sanford* (1857), which held that Congress was without constitutional power to prohibit slavery in the territories. The decision triggered violent controversy, foreclosed one avenue of compromise at the time, and helped to precipitate the Civil War. The decision has reasonably been called the most ignominious in the Supreme Court's history and is, baldly speaking, the only decision of the Court ever to be reversed by a war.

Between the Civil War and World War II, the Supreme Court can fairly be said to have been sympathetic to the concerns of business and industry at the expense of a wide variety of social legislation. The breaking point came with President Franklin D. Roosevelt's "court-packing plan" in 1937. From then on, the Court has shown great deference to congressional assertions of power in the field of social legislation.

This does not mean that the first third of this century was without enduring significance in terms of decisions made by the Court. During this period the Court laid the cornerstone for the development of a broad and active protection of civil liberties. Preeminent during this period in both the economic and civil liberties areas were two justices: Oliver Wendell Holmes (1902–32) and Louis D. Brandeis (1916–39). Their dissents, the former pithy and the latter compendious, in early cases concerning regulation of the economy and restrictions on fundamental freedoms eventually became the conventional wisdom.

The period immediately after World War II was neither a particularly active nor distinguished one for the Supreme Court. The arrival of Earl Warren as chief justice in 1953 coincided almost exactly with the Court's most far-reaching decision of the century—*Brown* v. *Board of Education* (1954). This decision, holding that separate but equal facilities for

In the unanimous Supreme Court decision, Swann v.
Charlotte-Mecklenburg Board of Education, *the Court
ruled that a court could order the busing of pupils to
overcome racial imbalance.*

Negroes in public schools violated the equal protection clause, created the greatest problem of compliance for the Court since Marshall's days. Despite changes in membership after Earl Warren retired as chief justice in 1969, the Court held firm to the principle of desegregation when it ruled unanimously in *Swann* v. *Charlotte-Mecklenburg Board of Education* (1971) that busing of pupils could be ordered by a court in order to overcome a racial imbalance that had resulted from segregation by law.

Other dramatically important decisions of the Warren Court involved the political process, freedom of the press, and the rights of criminal defendants. In *Baker* v. *Carr* (1962) and succeeding cases the Court invalidated, under the equal protection clause, grossly disproportionate state legislative districts. The political process was safeguarded in another way when the Court held in *New York Times Co.* v. *Sullivan* (1964) that freedom of the press protected a newspaper from liability to a public official for libel—provided that the falsehood was not published knowingly or intentionally. Perhaps the most controversial of the Warren Court decisions involved the criminal justice process. The Court required that evidence obtained in an unconstitutional search and seizure be excluded from trial, as in *Mapp* v. *Ohio* (1961), and that confessions obtained from an arrested person who did not have the benefit of counsel be similarly excluded, as in *Miranda* v. *Arizona* (1966).

Since the departure of Earl Warren, the Supreme Court has entered two highly controversial areas of constitutional adjudication: abortion and the death penalty. In *Roe* v. *Wade* (1972), the Court held that a woman had the right during the first trimester of pregnancy to decide with her doctor, free from state interference, whether to have an abortion. In *Furman* v. *Georgia* (1972), the death penalty was held invalid as "cruel and unusual punishment" in violation of the Eighth Amendment—at least as applied in a nonuniform and an unpredictable way. Four years later, in the wake of the Furman decision, the Court upheld more narrowly drawn statutes imposing the death penalty.

A Symbolic and Practical Role

The Supreme Court sits at the top of the American judicial system as the final arbiter of what the words of the Constitution mean. Its decisions affect the daily life of the country and serve as a check on the powers of other branches and levels

Convicts on death row read about the Supreme Court decision, Furman v. Georgia, *ruling that the death penalty is unconstitutional.*

of government. Yet, although the Court is, in effect, a policy-maker, it makes its decisions in the context of a specific dispute between two or more parties on the basis of a record of specific facts. This is one of the many built-in limitations on the Court's exercise of power. In addition to self-imposed canons of limitation, the Court also limits the effect, and ensures the legitimacy, of its decisions by providing written elaborations of its opinions—making known the reasons for the judgments it renders.

Moreover, in a practical way the Court holds itself open to reconsideration of doctrine in light of changed circumstances and fuller experience. This attitude, combined with a tradition of dissenting opinions, helps to inspire the people who make up its membership to clarify, refine, and test continually the working principles they create from the philosophic ideals written into the Constitution. Beyond its specific decisions and in light of the need to reach accommodation between absolutes, the symbolic function of the Court may be its most significant role in the life of the country.

5.
Administrative Law

Administrative law derives from the need to create and develop a system of public administration according to law, a concept comparable to the much older notion of justice according to law. Because administration involves the exercise of power by the executive arm of government, administrative law is important not only from a judicial standpoint but also from constitutional and political standpoints.

What Is Administrative Law?

There is no universally accepted definition of administrative law that adequately covers all the diverse systems that exist in the various states and the United States and in other countries. One convenient method of legal classification, however, defines each branch of law according to the subject matter that it regulates. Thus, administrative law is the law that regulates administration. This includes the organization, powers, duties, and functions of public authorities of all kinds who are engaged in administration; their relations with each other, with citizens, and with nongovernmental bodies; legal methods of controlling administration; and rights and liabilities of public officials.

The line between administrative and constitutional law is a vague one because these two types of law are complementary in many respects. The organization of the national legislature, the structure of the courts, the characteristics of the Cabinet, and the role of the head of state are generally regarded as matters of constitutional law in the broadest sense. Administrative law, on the other hand, is generally thought to embrace substantive and procedural provisions relating to the central government, as well as judicial review of administrative action. Some matters, such as the responsibility of government officials, however, cannot be exclusively assigned either to administrative law or to constitutional law. Some French and American jurists regard administrative law as including parts of constitutional law. This is one way of avoiding the dilemma.

In the United States the main emphasis in defining the scope of administrative law is placed on court decisions interpreting constitutional and statutory enactments and reviewing the administrative process. (In England, however, the principal stress is laid on the legislative, judicial, and executive powers of public authorities and on the safeguards provided for the protection of citizens' interests.)

The huge mass of substantive law relating to public health, education, housing, and other public services could logically be regarded as a part of the body of administrative law. But from a practical point of view, its sheer bulk makes the subject too unwieldy to master in a systematic manner. It is better, therefore, to consider these specialized bodies of law as ancillary branches (for example, the law of taxation or the law of public health) that can be used freely, when appropriate, to illustrate particular powers, functions, practices, or procedures applicable to administrative law.

Growth and Characteristics

The growth in the function of the state is a phenomenon that has occurred all over the world during the twentieth century. It may be found in both the more developed and the less developed areas, in both old and new countries, and in ideological systems of every kind. As a movement, it is far from reaching its zenith. With each addition to the functions of government, new powers have been acquired by the administrative organs concerned, whether part of the executive branch, of independent agencies, of local, regional, or state governments, or of special agencies created for a particular purpose. In the United States, the great growth of administrative agencies began in the 1930s with the New Deal of President Franklin D. Roosevelt. Today it would be difficult to describe the practical, everyday operation of the federal government without referring to the myriad departments, agencies, commissions, and bureaus through which it functions. The picture in the fifty states is similar.

Many functions of government have no exact counterpart in private activity. Traffic control, fire protection services, the arrest of criminals, environmental controls, the construction or repair of highways or mass transit systems, the provision of currency, town and country planning, excise taxes, customs, and innumerable other services are peculiar to government to a greater or lesser degree. In carrying out these functions the executive organs are assumed to represent the collective will of the community and to be acting for the common good. For this reason they are given powers not normally conferred on private persons. They are authorized

Executive Branch of the Government

The President of the United States

Executive Office of the President

The White House
Office of Management and Budget
Council of Economic Advisers
Council on Environmental Quality
Council on Wage and Price Stability
Domestic Policy Staff
National Security Council
Special Representative for Trade Negotiations
Office of Science and Technology Policy
Office of Administration

Departments

State	Commerce
Treasury	Labor
Defense	Health, Education, and Welfare
Justice	Housing and Urban Development
Interior	Transportation
Agriculture	Energy

Selected Agencies, Boards, and Commissions

Action	Central Intelligence Agency
Administrative Conference of the United States	Commission on Fine Arts
	Commission on Civil Rights
American Revolution Bicentennial Administration	Commodity Futures Trading Commission
American Battle Monuments Commission	Community Services Administration
Appalachian Regional Commission	Consumer Product Safety Commission
Civil Aeronautics Board	

Environmental Protection Agency

Equal Employment Opportunity Commission

Export Import Bank of the United States

Farm Credit Administration

Federal Communications Commission

Federal Deposit Insurance Corporation

Federal Election Commission

Federal Home Loan Bank Board

Federal Maritime Commission

Federal Mediation and Conciliation Service

Federal Trade Commission

Foreign Claims Settlement Commission

General Services Administration

Indian Claims Commission

Inter-American Foundation

Interstate Commerce Commission

National Aeronautics and Space Administration

National Capital Planning Commission

National Credit Union Administration

National Foundation of the Arts and Humanities

National Labor Relations Board

National Mediations Board

National Science Foundation

National Transportation Safety Board

Nuclear Regulatory Commission

Occupational Safety and Health Review Commission

Overseas Private Investment Corporation

Pension Benefit Guaranty Corporation

Postal Rate Commission

Railroad Retirement Board

Renegotiation Board

Securities and Exchange Commission

Selective Service System

Small Business Administration

Smithsonian Institution

Tennessee Valley Authority

U.S. Arms Control and Disarmament Agency

U.S. Civil Service Commission

United States International Trade Commission

United States Postal Service

Veterans Administration

Water Resources Council

to require citizens to surrender their property rights, upon the showing of a proper public purpose, and they may restrict individual freedom of action in many different ways, ranging from the quarantining of the sick to the detaining of suspected criminals. To take another example, a public authority in the course of building houses or clearing a slum is in a different, and much stronger, legal position and enjoys certain advantages over a speculative builder or a private developer who is engaged in similar operations.

Distinguishing public administration from private action, one could say that administrative law differs significantly from private law in that the latter regulates the actions, interests, and obligations of private persons and businesses. Public administration employees enjoy a special status whereby they are entitled to certain procedural protections in connection with hiring and firing. For example, taxes are not "ordinary debts," and the governmental forces of public administration are not limited in their collection efforts to the law relating to the recovery of debts by private persons. The interrelations between executive organs and their relations with private in-

The growth in the function of government on the local, regional, state, and federal levels is a twentieth-century phenomenon. Mass transit systems are one of the many services that are peculiar to government.

dividuals are usually regulated by compulsory or permissive powers that the legislature has conferred upon the executive organs.

Administrative law encompasses two distinct areas of concern: the internal and external aspects of administration. The former include such matters as the relations between the government and its officials, between a local authority and its committees, and between a central executive department and a local or state authority. The external aspects of public administration, on the other hand, deal with the relations between the administrative agencies and private persons or outside interests. In practice, the internal and external aspects are often closely interwoven. Legal provisions of both kinds frequently exist side by side in the same statute. Thus, a law dealing with education may modify the administrative organization of the education service and may also regulate the relations between parents and school authorities.

A distinction can be made between the type of administrative law that consists of a command addressed by legislation to the citizen, requiring him to act or to refrain from acting in a certain way, and the type that consists of a direction addressed to the administrative authorities telling them how they must or may act. When a rule of administrative law takes the form of an unconditional command addressed to the citizen, there is usually a criminal penalty or a stiff civil fine attached to its violation. Heavy penalties, for example, often result from violations of clean air or water standards or occupational health and safety regulations. The application of the penalty may be entrusted to the criminal courts or to an administrative agency. The courts, however, can review any administrative action that is the subject of a complaint in the course of an enforcement proceeding.

Statutory directions addressed to the executive authorities may impose absolute duties, or they may confer discretionary powers on the agency, authorizing it to take action of a specified kind in certain circumstances if it wishes. There are many variations of these types. Legislation may be passed, for example, giving general directions for the executive bodies to follow in establishing or operating a system of factory inspection, a policy of slum clearance, or a comprehensive city planning scheme. The statute establishes the conditions under which it will be lawful for the agency to act and clothes the authorities with the necessary powers, which often involve considerable discretion.

In this kind of legislation the task of the executive is not confined merely to carrying out the directions of the legislature. Instead, the executive often shares in the lawmaking process itself by being empowered to issue rules, regulations, or orders dealing with particular matters not expressly governed by the statute. This is all part of the ordinary process through which legislative powers are delegated by the legislature to inferior lawmaking bodies. It may be viewed also as an essential feature of modern government, necessary because many matters are too technical, too detailed, too subject to frequent change, or too dependent on unforeseen circumstances to be included in the main body of legislation, which is more difficult to change than are individual regulations.

Whatever the source of the rule-making power of the executive may be, it must have safeguards to ensure that it is properly used. Regulations must not exceed the scope of the delegated powers. They must also be consistent with the aims of the parent statute. Whenever practicable, persons and interest groups likely to be affected by proposed rules should be consulted before the rules take effect. Finally, regulations must not contradict relevant constitutional and legal standards. In most instances, regulations are reviewed by the head of the appropriate executive department and are required to be published during a certain period of time before they come into force. Occasionally, Congress or a state legislature will reserve the right to veto proposed regulations. As a practical matter, however, the first close scrutiny of a regulation may occur in a lawsuit brought in an ordinary court.

Public administration consists of the execution of public policy by public authorities. It represents, therefore, the means by which the purposes of the government are promoted and realized in action. Administrative law is the legal framework within which public administration operates. One of its chief aims is to ensure efficient, economical, and just administration. A system of administrative law that impedes or frustrates administration is obviously inefficient, and a system that results in injustice to the individual is surely undesirable. How can anyone judge whether administrative law helps or hinders effective administration, however, or works in ways that deny justice to the individual? One can only examine the ends that public administration is supposed to serve as well as the means that it employs.

In this connection it is possible to speak only in the broad-

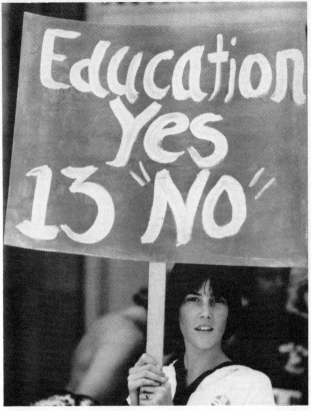

Despite the concern over the possibility of diminished services, Proposition 13, a proposal to cut property taxes, passed by an overwhelming majority in California. The only way to reconcile the drastic loss in revenue with the maintenance of adequate services is to make the government more efficient.

est generalities. One might say that one aim of all governments—regardless of the economic and political system or stage of development—is to achieve a high rate of economic growth and a higher average income or standard of living per person. Most governments today are pursuing goals of modernization, urbanization, and industrialization. Most are trying also to provide major social services, especially those of education and public health, at as high a standard as possible.

Because of these ambitious goals, the level of popular expectation is much higher now than it was in former times. Governments today are expected to achieve progress as well as to maintain order. There is a widespread belief that wise and well-directed government action can help to abolish poverty, prevent severe unemployment, raise the standard of living of a country, and bring about rapid social development. (The belief, however, has come under increasing attack during the 1970s in several countries, as expectations generated by the social programs of the 1960s have not been fully realized over the short term.) Despite some disillusionment with government's ability to change things for the better, people are far more aware than their forefathers were of the impact of government on their daily lives and of its potential for good and evil.

Bureaucracy and Its Problems

As governmental functions have expanded, bureaucracy has grown—an inevitable consequence. Both federal and state agencies in the United States have proliferated, touching more and more areas of daily life. There has been a corresponding increase in the number of government officials and employees, along with an expansion of the scope and depth of their powers. The breadth of the powers of government officials highlights the dilemma between the necessity of selecting qualified people and at the same time appointing officials whose policy views are consistent with the administration's. Merit selection through the Civil Service is the rule rather than the exception for all but the highest

positions in the federal government. Many states, in contrast, still tolerate political patronage to a large degree.

Bureaucratic maladies take many different forms. They include overdevotion to precedent, remoteness from the rest of the community, inaccessibility, arrogance in dealing with the general public, ineffective organization, waste of manpower, procrastination, an excessive sense of self-importance, indifference to the feelings or convenience of citizens, an overblown sense of institutional loyalty, inflexibility, abuse of power, and a reluctance to admit error. Although most U.S. administrative agencies were originally created with the purpose of serving the public interest in a certain area, many of them have been criticized for becoming the pawns of the very industries they should be regulating.

A wide range of techniques is available to deal with these problems. Some defects, of course, can be prevented or cured by good management and careful training. A number of approaches may prove useful in this connection, including work-study programs, on-the-job training, more sophisticated organization and management methods, operations research, social surveys, and public relations. Other defects require different, and more subtle, correctional devices. It has been suggested, for example, that a regulatory agency that is controlled by those whom it regulates might require a new watchdog agency dedicated to consumer protection to serve the public interest. Devices such as the Freedom of Information Act and open-meetings laws have been introduced to make administrative agencies more accessible to the ordinary citizen and thus more accountable. Finally, reorganizing and consolidating certain agencies often eliminates many of the problems of an entrenched bureaucracy.

The Role of Administrative Law

Administrative law itself can make a valuable contribution in controlling bureaucracy. In order to understand some of the ways in which administrative law interacts with the larger system of government, it is helpful to consider this type of law from three different perspectives: agency relations with legislative bodies, normal agency operations, and judicial review of administrative action.

Agency Relations with Legislative Bodies. The role of legislative bodies in shaping administrative law does not end with the enactment of the statute that created the agency. Congress or a state legislature exercises continuing influence over the administrative process in a variety of ways. An obvious control device is the power to appropriate funds and include restrictive riders on appropriations bills.

In addition to this direct control, legislatures may establish "oversight" committees, which are given the task of monitoring the work of a particular agency or department. Legislative hearings often provide an informal vehicle for control by the legislative branch.

Normal Agency Operations. Within newly created agencies two distinct roles are usually played. The first concerns questions of policy and usually takes the form of rule making. The second involves the application of policies or rules to particular situations—such as license proceedings or proceedings to resolve complaints about statutory or regulatory violations.

In their policymaking role, agencies frequently hold public hearings and solicit written comments on proposed actions. They may also hold hearings and seek written comments in the course of adjudicatory or licensing proceedings through the device of intervention. This device permits an interested person or group to participate to a greater or lesser degree in the proceedings. Both rule making and adjudication contribute to the building up of a coherent body of agency law in the area of the agency's expertise. Often an agency permits an appeal from the decision of a lower official to a higher official or to the agency as a whole; this also helps to keep the law uniform. The Internal Revenue Service, for example, provides for several administrative appeals before a dissatisfied taxpayer must turn to the courts for relief.

Judicial Review of Administrative Action. Judicial review of administrative action is, nevertheless, the heart of administrative law. Many aspects of an official decision or an administrative act may be scrutinized by the judicial process: the competence of the public authority; the extent of its legal powers; the adequacy and fairness of the procedure; the evidence considered in arriving at the administrative decision and the motives underlying it; and the nature and scope of the discretionary power. An administrative act or decision can be invalidated on any of these grounds, if the reviewing court or tribunal has sufficiently wide jurisdiction.

In the federal government and most of the states there is a presumption that administrative action can always be reviewed judicially although a specific statute may direct otherwise. Beyond this, there is also the question of responsibility for the damage caused by the public authority in the performance of its duties. Lastly, the court must determine what type of relief should be ordered: injunctive relief, monetary compensation, or some combination of the two.

Development of Judicial Review

The nature and extent of the judicial review of administrative action and the institutions through which it is undertaken vary greatly among the countries of the world. The prevailing system in the United States is derived from the English common-law model.

In England the constitutional struggle in the seventeenth century played a decisive part in determining the relations between the courts and the executive. The Stuart kings came into open conflict with judges over the judges' right to decide questions affecting the royal power and even their right to pronounce an independent judgment in cases in which the king had an interest. Francis Bacon, in his essay *Of Judicature* (1612), expressed the Royalist point of view when he declared that the judges should be "lions, but yet lions under the throne." "It is a happy thing in a State," he wrote, "when Kings and States do often consult with Judges, and again, when Judges do often consult with the King and State: the one, when there is matter of law intervenient in business of state; the other, when there is some consideration of state intervenient in matter of law." Sir Edward Coke, Bacon's great rival, who refused to comply with the wishes of James I in a number of cases where the royal prerogative was involved, strongly resisted the subordination of the judiciary to the royal will. The king, nonetheless, harangued the judges repeatedly on their duty to respect the royal prerogative and power.

In the seventeenth-century constitutional conflict the judges and lawyers joined Parliament in opposing Charles I. An essential feature of the settlement was the establishment of the independence of the judges. From that time on, there was to be one system of law to which all English subjects would owe obedience. Certain consequences followed from this solution. First, the executive possessed no inherent powers other than the carefully defined and limited prerogatives of the crown, which were recognized by the law. Second, the judges were expected to protect the subjects from the executive. A more intangible consequence was the spread of the belief that "organized government" and "law" were opposed to one another. The conflict between James I and the judges survived in an antagonism between the legal profession and the executive, particularly the civil service.

These developments established the principle that the executive should never interfere with the judiciary in its exercise of judicial functions. This was almost the only strict application in England of the doctrine of the separation of powers. On the other hand, it was regarded as right and proper that the judiciary should interfere with the executive whenever a minister or a department was shown to have acted illegally. In this way, the concept of the rule of law came gradually to be identified with the idea that judges, in ordinary legal proceedings in ordinary courts, had the power to rule upon the lawfulness of the activities of the executive. Any attempt to distinguish between public and private law was resisted by the generations brought up on this traditional view as an effort to destroy the universality of the law and the power of the judges to keep the executive within bounds.

The principle that all public authorities are subject to having the lawfulness of their acts and decisions tested in the courts was applied in the countries to which the English common law was transplanted. In the United States this conception prevailed, despite the much stricter interpretation of the doctrine of the separation of powers adopted by the founding fathers and the embodiment of that doctrine in both the federal and state constitutions. The framers of the federal Constitution did not consider a complete separation of powers to be feasible. They therefore modified the doctrine by adding to it the notion of "checks and balances," whereby each of the three branches of government would be restrained by the others. Actually, this strengthened the power of the courts to review the actions of the executive, due to the eventual acceptance of the power of the judiciary as the ultimate arbiter of all constitutional and statutory disputes.

The common-law system has been extensively modified in the United States in the twentieth century. It never corresponded with the realities of the situation in England. Prior to the Crown Proceedings Act of 1947, it was not possible to sue ministers and their departments in tort (claiming civil or private wrong by act or omission) because of the legal doctrine that "the king can do no wrong." Sovereign immunity, as the doctrine is commonly called, also barred tort suits against the federal government in the United States until the Federal Tort Claims Act, which waived the government's immunity in many kinds of cases, was passed in 1949. Many states also have tort claims acts that are similar to the federal law.

In England the development of social services has been accompanied by the creation of a large number of administrative tribunals to hear and determine disputes between a government department and a citizen. The jurisdiction of these tribunals is specialized and narrowly circumscribed. It relates to such functions as social insurance, social assistance, national health, rent control, assessment of property for local taxation, the compulsory acquisition of land by public authorities, and the registration of children's homes. There are about two thousand of these tribunals.

Since 1958 a permanent Council on Tribunals appointed by the lord chancellor has exercised a general supervision over them, but they remain unsystematic and uncoordinated. They exist because they offer a method of administrative adjudication that is far cheaper, more informal, and faster than that offered by the courts. Their members are persons with specialized knowledge and experience. The strict and complex rules of evidence that prevail in the courts need not be followed; these tribunals have acquired general approval for the quality and impartiality of their work. Appeals on questions of law consist in most instances in taking the administrative tribunal's decision to the High Court. There is still no comprehensive administrative jurisdiction in England to provide an opportunity for judicial review over the whole field of executive action and decision.

In the United States the courts have been much more far-reaching and comprehensive in reviewing administrative action than have their English counterparts. Nevertheless, a significant amount of adjudication is now performed by the agencies themselves, rather than by courts of law.

The movement toward administrative tribunals in the United States began with the Interstate Commerce Act of 1887, which established the Interstate Commerce Commission to regulate and control railways and other carriers. The law introduced a new type of federal agency outside the framework of the executive departments, with a large measure of independence from the president. This was followed by a number of other regulatory commissions of a similar type, including the Federal Trade Commission, the Federal Power Commission, the Federal Communications Commission, the Securities and Exchange Commission, the Civil

Aeronautics Board, and the National Labor Relations Board. Congress has delegated administrative, legislative, and judicial functions to these bodies. The Securities and Exchange Commission, for example, supervises the operation of stock exchanges and specific public distributions of new securities. It also issues rules and regulations designed generally to govern transactions in securities, and it may impose administrative sanctions on persons who violate certain provisions of the securities laws. In the past the Supreme Court occasionally found laws that delegated legislative responsibilities to administrative agencies unconstitutional, as a violation of the principle of the separation of powers. The Court has not done so, however, since the 1935 case of *Schechter Poultry Corp.* v. *United States*, which invalidated the National Industrial Recovery Act of 1933. It seems likely that challenges to delegation of powers to administrative agencies will continue to be unsuccessful.

The scope of judicial review in the federal government and most of the states is determined primarily by legislation, which may confer a right of appeal to a court from the decision or act of a public authority, or, conversely, may exclude or limit such an appeal. Legislation may specify certain matters, such as what court is authorized to hear the appeal, what points may be raised in the appeal, what

Contemporary cartoons depict the birth (left) and the death (right) of the National Recovery Agency. The National Industrial Recovery Act, under which the agency was created, was declared unconstitutional by a Supreme Court ruling in 1935.

prerequisites to the right of appeal exist, and who may take the appeal. The governing legislation, therefore, sets certain limits on appeals of administrative action. But the judiciary itself can determine to a considerable extent the circumstances under which the courts will or will not review the action. Thus, in the United States the refusal by the State Department to issue a passport has been subjected to review by the Supreme Court. In contrast, in the United Kingdom such a question would almost certainly be held to be nonreviewable. The U.S. courts, however, will not review administrative decisions that are not final, nor will they review cases that have become "moot"—that is, cases in which the original controversy has been resolved in some other way. In laying down the limits within which judicial review is available, convention, judicial precedent, and a reluctance to depart from the legal doctrines applicable to private litigation can be significant influences.

A wide variety of causes may give rise to claims for which remedies are available: for example, the failure of a public agency to perform a duty properly; the failure to discharge the duty at all; corrupt motives; and the use of improper or unauthorized means. Usually, in order to invoke the process of judicial review it is necessary to claim that a public authority has committed a culpable fault of some kind and that this has resulted in injury to the claimant. For the most part, the doctrine of "liability without fault" does not represent the governing rule in American administrative law. Workmen's compensation boards and occupational health and safety commissions may represent limited exceptions. In the normal situation, in which fault of some kind must be proved, a wide range of remedies can be used against erring public authorities. In appropriate cases, the courts have overruled administrative decisions, invalidated unlawful regulations, issued declaratory judgments defining the rights of parties, awarded monetary relief, and prohibited or demanded action.

The most difficult problem in administrative law is the control of administrative discretion. Although there are certain legal requirements that must be observed in exercising discretionary powers, the courts have frequently declared that they may not substitute their own decision for that of a public authority to which the discretion has been given. In other words, the courts will inquire into and invalidate administrative acts that were not authorized by the governing statutes, or were taken in bad faith, or were arbitrary, capricious, or unreasonable; but they will not revise or replace a decision simply because they believe it was unwise or inexpedient. Furthermore, the courts usually confine their inquiry to the evidence and arguments that were originally made before the administrative agency.

Administrative Procedure

The administrative state is characterized by a wide range of subject matter areas touched by administrative agencies and also by the existence of a sophisticated administrative process. The essence of the process is an orderly and ascertainable procedure, which may be prescribed by legislation or regulations laid down by the courts or specified by the administrative authority itself or by a higher level of government.

Fair and reliable procedures are of great importance to the administrative system. They make it possible to fix responsibility on a particular official or body at each stage of the administrative process. They can safeguard the rights of citizens and protect the executive departments against charges of arbitrary action. They can ensure regularity and consistency in the handling of individual cases. Much depends, of course, on the quality and purpose of the procedural requirements.

The federal government's model for all administrative procedure is the Administrative Procedure Act, passed originally in 1946. The act applies chiefly to each authority of the government, except the Congress, the courts, the territorial governments, and the government of the District of Columbia. Two kinds of procedures are spelled out in detail in the act: rule making and adjudication. When an agency wants to establish a general rule or regulation, it must publish a notice describing the proposal in the Federal Register and give interested persons an opportunity to participate in the decision—either by submitting written comments or by presenting oral statements, as the agency elects. Once the proposed rule or regulation becomes effective, it is published again in the Federal Register. A complete set of each agency's rules and regulations is published yearly in the Code of Federal Regulations.

Adjudicatory proceedings resemble trials in many ways. An administrative law judge usually presides over the hearing; interested parties submit their versions of the relevant facts and legal arguments, and written decisions are issued explaining the agency's action. Licensing proceedings follow the adjudicatory model. The Administrative Procedure Act also gives a right to judicial review to any person adversely affected by an agency's action, unless some other law contains contrary provisions.

Some states have followed the federal example and enacted administrative procedure acts of their own, patterned largely after the federal act. Other states, however, continue to approach problems of administrative procedure on an agency-by-agency basis. The powers of administrative agencies vary widely from state to state and within individual states; similarly, the scope of judicial review available differs considerably.

General concepts of fairness and due process have strongly influenced the development of administrative procedure in the United States. Since the passage of the Administrative Procedure Act, more organized efforts have been made to streamline and improve administrative procedures. Among the groups working toward this end is the Administrative Conference of the United States, established by statute to oversee the various federal agencies and departments and to recommend needed reforms. The Conference is composed of from seventy-five to ninety-one persons, a majority of whom are representatives from the executive branch and the agencies. The organized bar has also taken an interest in the continued improvement of administrative procedure, on both national and state levels.

Good administrative procedure is of great value, but it is always possible to exaggerate its importance. The substantive correctness of any decision made by an administrative agency is more critically important because the factual accuracy of an agency's conclusions is rarely subjected to judicial review. This is particularly true in the case of agencies that deal with complex scientific problems, such as the Nuclear Regulatory Commission or the Environmental Protection Agency: here the courts lack the expertise to decide whether or not the agency's conclusion was correct.

Normally, the primary question to be decided when an administrative decision is reviewed is whether or not the correct procedure was observed. Little or no attention is paid to the substance of the decision. Courts in the United States ask only if the agency's decision was supported by "substantial evidence," viewing the record as a whole. If the evidence is not sufficient or if the agency has failed to satisfy some procedural requirement, the court ordinarily sends the case back to the agency for further proceedings.

Judicial review, whether conducted by administrative tribunals or the ordinary courts, is the most appropriate way for taking such actions as inquiring into the legal competence of a public authority and the fairness and adequacy of its procedure; the evidence on which it relied in a particular case and the motives or considerations on which it was based; and the extent of the grant of any discretionary power it may possess. Because there is such a great disparity between the agency's expertise and the court's, judicial review is less effective as a method of inquiring into the wisdom, expediency, or reasonableness of administrative acts. Past action has shown that courts and tribunals are unwilling to substitute their own decisions for those of the responsible authorities. But in some instances the law that allows judicial review entitles the complaining party to a "trial de novo" (a new trial) in the reviewing court. In this situation, the agency's decision is set aside entirely, and the court retries the entire case. The other extreme of judicial review occurs when the courts have virtually no authority to review discretionary powers. With only a few narrow exceptions, this is the case with decisions that have been made by Selective Service boards and other military administrative tribunals.

It is, of course, impracticable to subject every administrative act or decision to investigation or review. This would slow up the work of government to an unacceptable degree. The person complaining must therefore always present sufficient facts to show that some form of maladministration has occurred to convince the court that further inquiry should take place.

It is true that administrative tribunals and courts can annul unlawful decisions, allow appeals, declare the law, impose fines, and award damages. Technically speaking, however, they cannot compel the government to act in a particular way, because sanctions cannot be imposed on the government in its sovereign capacity unless it has expressly given its permission. Such courts do have the power to direct injunctions, orders for specific performance, and orders for writs of mandamus (specifically directing the performance of a legal duty) against government officials in appropriate circumstances. Thus, sovereign immunity is rarely a bar to effective relief.

The Ombudsman

The type of official for civil affairs known in Scandinavia as an ombudsman is not as yet widespread in the United States. But local governments, state universities, and other smaller public institutions are beginning to experiment with the use of ombudsmen. It is therefore interesting to explore in some detail what this office does, since it offers one way to keep administrative agencies responsive to public needs.

Originating in Sweden, the office of ombudsman was created by the constitution of 1809. The holder of this high post—ombudsman for civil affairs—is appointed by Parliament. He enjoys complete independence and is responsible only to the law.

The Swedish ombudsman is entrusted with the duty of supervising the entire sphere of civil affairs, including the judiciary, the police, prisons, and both central and local administrative agencies. He can act as a public prosecutor and as a receiver of complaints from aggrieved citizens. He also acts as an inspector undertaking careful investigations into such institutions as jails, mental hospitals, homes for delinquent children, and alcoholic rehabilitation clinics to discover if they are being administered lawfully. In the past the ombudsman was mainly concerned with errors of one kind or another in the courts, such as delay, improper conduct, and other internal faults. Now, by contrast, the bulk of his work is directed to the civil administration. A separate ombudsman supervises military affairs.

Apart from occasional prosecutions, the ombudsman has little positive power other than the right to inspect and to demand the fullest information. But he is entitled to comment, criticize, and make recommendations as to the correct interpretation of the law. He can recommend that the government pay compensation to a complainant. He can propose changes in the law. He can expose maladministration in whatever form or wherever it takes place. Only ministers and the king are immune from his penetrating scrutiny.

The office of ombudsman was created with the intention that its holder would safeguard the rights of the citizen and the interests of the Swedish people by protecting them from the shortcomings to which even the best system of government is liable. The experience of a century and a half in Sweden has proved the usefulness of the institution there.

The other Scandinavian countries have followed the Swedish example, as have Finland, New Zealand, Great Britain, West Germany, and the province of Alberta in Canada. Public interest in the idea, aroused in other countries, appears to be growing in the United States. There are, however, considerable differences in the powers and the status given the ombudsmen in these countries.

In countries where the ombudsman office has been established, it is regarded as a part of the system of administrative law that scrutinizes the work of the executive. The ombudsman is the appointee of the legislative branch and not of the executive. (In a limited way, the General Accounting Office of the U.S. Congress serves this function.) The ombudsman's function is to safeguard citizens' interests by ensuring administration according to law, discovering instances where the administrative process has failed, and eliminating such breakdowns by various methods. He may bring pressure to bear on the responsible authority, publicize a refusal to rectify injustice or a defective administrative practice or bring the matter to the attention of the legislature, or institute a criminal prosecution or disciplinary action. There can be no doubt about the ombudsman's value to the countries in which the office has been established.

Part of the ombudsman's usefulness lies in his ability to reassure citizens who believe that they have been unjustly treated that a careful inquiry into their complaints shows them to be groundless. In the United States, private groups such as Common Cause or public interest research groups have served this function to a limited degree. They lack many of the official powers of the ombudsman, however, and hence cannot be as effective as a statutory official in many situations.

Toward Better Administrative Law

Most of this survey has been concerned with the control of public administration by methods other than those regarded as political—such as popular elections, legislative control of the executive, and pressure groups. The justification for this emphasis is that, as the powers of the administrative state increase in scope and depth, the need to safeguard the rights and interests of citizens, both individually and collectively, also becomes greater. The safeguards concern both the rights of the individual in his dealings with the powerful machinery of contemporary government and the interest of the community in ensuring that administration is carried on according to law. None of the methods of legal scrutiny, control, and prescription described is intended to undermine the strength, effectiveness, and vigor of the administrative state, except where such interference is necessary to protect the individual's constitutional or statutory rights. Methods of scrutiny, furthermore, reveal the shortcomings of an administrative system and suggest remedies for those defects.

Administrative law can make the activities of the modern state more acceptable to the citizen in several ways. It can prevent or correct maladministration, lay down standards of behavior for government officials, insist on just procedures, refuse to permit the abuse of discretionary powers, and ensure that equality of treatment is a condition of legality. By becoming more acceptable to the citizens, public administration can operate more efficiently and at the same time deliver more needed services to the people.

6.
Taxation

An income tax, in the generally accepted meaning of the term, is a tax imposed on net income—the total income less certain expenses incurred in earning it. The tax may apply to individuals (personal income tax), corporations (corporate income tax), or both. A net income tax can be distinguished from a gross income tax, which applies to the entire gross income of individuals, corporations, or both, without any deduction of the expenses of gaining the income, or other items. The personal income tax usually applies only to income in excess of a certain figure, and thus low-income groups are freed from the tax.

Income tax rates may be the same at all income levels, but they are more commonly progressive, the rate rising as the size of the income rises. Progression (or graduation, as it is sometimes called) is particularly common with personal income taxes.

Development

Income taxation developed slowly, with many reverses. The advantages of income taxation were recognized centuries ago, but fear that administration would be difficult or impossible delayed its widespread use. The growth in revenue needs as government expenditures increased, particularly during wars, and the increasing acceptance of the view that government should use its fiscal powers to reduce inequality in the distribution of income gave impetus to the income tax movement. Introduction of the tax was facilitated by the increased importance of exchange and the earning of money incomes, more adequate record keeping, the use of banking facilities, and improved standards of tax administration.

Limited attempts to use income taxes were made by four states early in the nineteenth century. But the administration was weak and the yield was very low. Although additional states attempted to use the tax prior to 1900, the first successful state use was the Wisconsin tax in 1911. Other states then followed, although the expanding use by the states was slowed after 1940 by the high federal tax. By 1978, however, more than forty states had adopted income taxes, many of which conform closely with the federal income tax. Local government units, especially in Pennsylvania, Ohio, and Michigan, also use income taxes; often they are restricted to salaries and wages. During the 1960s local governments in some states imposed a surcharge on the state tax on their residents.

The first federal income tax was imposed in 1862 to meet Civil War expenditures. The rate, at first 3%, was later raised, made progressive for a time, and then returned to a 10% figure in 1865; exemptions were provided. Despite the lack of adequate enforcement, the tax yielded substantial revenue. Complaints of evasion and the dislike of many groups for the principle of the tax, however, led Congress to allow it to expire in 1872.

During the succeeding decades the tax remained a political issue, support coming primarily from farm and labor groups. In 1894 a 2% tax was imposed, in part to offset revenue losses from tariff reductions. In a reversal of the Civil War tax decision, the 1894 tax was held to be unconstitutional by the Supreme Court on the grounds that certain portions of it were direct taxes and were therefore invalid because the tax was not apportioned according to population as required by the Constitution. An immediate attempt was made to sanction income taxation by a constitutional amendment. This effort culminated in the adoption of the Sixteenth Amendment, which became effective in 1913. Meanwhile, in 1909, a levy had been successfully imposed upon corporation profits in the technical form of an excise tax.

In 1913, immediately after the Sixteenth Amendment became effective, Congress enacted a personal income tax, with a normal rate of 1% on income in excess of $3,000 for a single person and of $4,000 for a married person, and surtax rates ranging from 1% to 6% on taxable incomes in excess of $20,000. The corporate rate was 1%. The development of the tax after 1913 can be summarized briefly, in terms of the following major trends:

1. *Sharp increases during World War I.* In 1918 the normal rate was made progressive, with a range from 6% to 12%, and the progression of the surtax was greatly sharpened, the rate rising from 1% to 65%. The combined normal and surtax rate on income in excess of $1 million was 77%, the highest rate used in any country to that date. Exemptions were also lowered.

2. *Gradual reductions in rates and increases in exemptions during the 1920s.* The exemption reached $1,500 for

single persons and $3,500 for married persons, with $400 for other dependents, by 1925. The normal tax was lowered to a range of from ½% to 4%, and the top surtax rate was lowered to 20%.

3. **Increases during the 1930s.** In an effort to reduce budget deficits, the exemption for married couples was lowered to $2,500, and the basic rate was raised to 4% in 1932; progression was sharply increased in an effort to place more of the burden on the higher income groups. Later in the period the surtax rates were raised to a maximum of 75%.

4. **Drastic increases during World War II.** At the beginning of World War II the tax was converted almost overnight from a "rich man's tax" to one that reached the great majority of workers. The exemption, after several reductions, was set at a flat $500 per person, including the taxpayer; and the surtax rate was made to apply to all taxable income, the initial tax rate reaching 23%. The maximum combined normal and surtax rate reached 94%. The normal and surtax rates were

"Oh, Grandma, what big teeth you have!"

eventually consolidated into a single rate. The number of returns, which had been six million in 1937, reached fifty million in 1945, or 38% of the population. In 1943 a significant change was made in the methods of collection by the establishment of the withholding system on wages and salaries.

5. **Modifications.** In the postwar period, continuing high expenditures prevented sharp reductions in the income tax. The general level, while fluctuating, remained much closer to the wartime figures than to those of the 1930s. Several modifications were made, however, in the structure of the tax.

The rates were reduced in 1946 to a basic figure of 19% and a maximum of 86.45%. In 1948 the exemption figure was raised to $600 per person, the rates were reduced again (the basic rate to 16.6%), and the splitting of income between a husband and wife was universally permitted. This rule greatly reduced the operation of progressively higher rates for married couples, because of the fact that, in the typical family unit at that time, only one spouse was a wage earner. During the Korean War (1950–53) the rates were raised again, to a high of 22.2% basic and 92% maximum. In 1953 the rate increase was eliminated, and the basic rate table with rates ranging from 20% to 91% was restored. In 1954 a number of other modifications were made, primarily to ease the severity of various rules relating to dependents, to working wives, to depreciation, and to other questions. A step was also taken to reduce the double taxation of dividend income. In 1964 Congress reduced the tax rates, with an initial rate of 14% and a maximum of 70%. In 1968 a surcharge of 10% of the existing tax liability was added. The surcharge was eliminated for the taxable years 1971 and those following.

The corporate income tax followed a pattern somewhat similar to the personal tax. The rate, originally 1%, reached a high of 13.5% in 1926, was reduced to 12% in 1928, and was raised again in the 1930s. During the 1930s limited rate progression was introduced, primarily to lessen the adverse effects of the tax on the growth of small businesses. In 1936, for example, the beginning rate was 8%, the maximum 15%. Subjecting the dividend income of individuals to both the normal and surtax rates in 1936 established a double taxation of corporate dividend income. A proposal to apply the corporate tax only to undistributed profits was rejected by Congress in favor of a supplementary tax on such profits in addition to the regular levy. This tax led to great protests and was abandoned in 1937.

Taxes in the United States

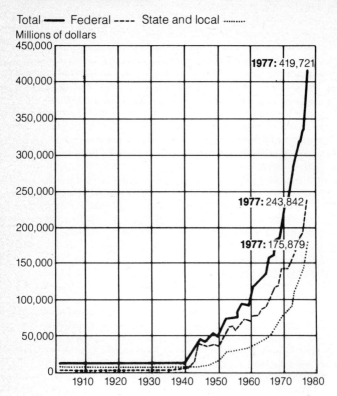

Total —— Federal ---- State and local ········

Millions of dollars

1977: 419,721

1977: 243,842

1977: 175,879

During World War II the corporate income tax was raised drastically, the maximum rate reaching 40%. The structure of the tax was greatly simplified in 1946 with the establishment of a two-rate structure, a 23% rate applying to all corporate income, and a surtax rate of 19% on income in excess of $25,000. The basic rate was raised to 28% in 1951 and to 30% in 1952, the maximum effective rate being 52%. The 1964 tax reduction lowered the basic rate to 22%, the maximum to 48%. A 10% surcharge on the existing tax was added in 1968 but was eliminated for the taxable years 1971 and those following. Later, the basic rate was lowered to 20%, with the maximum remaining at 48%. In 1978 the Revenue

Act of that year created a five-rate corporate tax table, with a new basic rate of 17% and a new maximum of 46%.

The Tax Reform Act of 1969 made numerous changes in specific features of both individual and corporate income taxes. It also provided increases in the number of personal exemptions and the standard deduction. The Revenue Act of 1978 provided an $18.7 billion tax cut that was in many ways a major departure from other tax cuts by Democratic congresses in the preceding fifteen years, in that most of the benefits would go to taxpayers in the upper-income brackets. In all, the measure contained $13.1 billion in reductions for individuals, providing an average 7.2% tax cut—most of it concentrated in the $15,000 to $50,000 brackets. Also included were sizable cuts in capital gains taxes and in business taxes.

Practical Aspects

Under the new law, beginning Jan. 1, 1979, the minimum income for which a tax return must be filed was increased to $3,300 for a single person and a head of household, and to $5,400 for a married couple under age 65 filing a joint return. The 1978 tax legislation also reduced the then-prevailing table of 25 income brackets to 15 (16 for single persons). The brackets were widened to achieve this simplification, but the rates assigned to each bracket continue to range from 14% to 70%

If the income to be reported on the return (Form 1040) is under a specified amount, consisting only of wages and salaries and not more than a small amount of dividends or interest, and if the taxpayer elects to take the standard deduction (now known as the zero bracket amount) rather than to itemize his deductions, only the first page of the return need be completed (or a short form can be filed); the tax liability can be determined by referring to tax tables supplied with the return instructions. Moreover, if the adjusted gross income reported on the return is $20,000 or less and consists only of wages, salaries, tips, dividends, interest, pensions, and annuities, and if the taxpayer elects the zero bracket amount, the taxpayer might choose to have the Internal Revenue Service compute his tax for him.

The normal filing date is April 15. Married couples may file separate or joint returns, but the latter is often preferable because it provides an automatic splitting of income between the two persons. However, if the two married people earn approximately the same amount, the advantage disappears, and they are actually paying a "marriage tax."

Gross Income. The law does not define income, but the regulations indicate the types of items that must be included in gross income. These include all income in the usual sense, including the gross receipts of the operators of business firms, professionals, and farmers. Receipts that involve merely a change in the form of wealth with no increase in value do not constitute income. Increases in the value of property are taxed only when they are realized through the sale of the property, and at that time they receive special treatment.

Among the items of income specifically excluded are most veterans' benefits, Social Security benefits, gifts and inheritances, some casualty insurance benefits, life insurance benefits upon death, and interest on state and municipal bonds. Partial exclusion is permitted for sick-leave pay, and a small amount of corporate dividends received is exempt.

Business Deductions and Adjusted Gross Income. In general, various expenses incurred in gaining the income, known as business deductions, may be subtracted from the gross income to determine the adjusted gross income. These are of primary importance for people such as operators of business firms, professionals operating their own practices, and farmers.

All business and trade expenses, in the usual sense of the term, are deductible, including depreciation on capital equipment and interest on borrowed money. Depreciation deductions must conform with regulations relating to the length of the life of the property and to allocation formulas. For an employee, business deductions are allowed for unreimbursed travel expenses (including meals and lodging while away from home) that are undertaken in the service of an employer, and deductions are also allowed for certain moving expenses.

Nonbusiness Deductions. From the adjusted gross income the taxpayer may deduct certain personal expenses, which are designated as nonbusiness deductions. These include:

a. Contributions to religious, medical, and educational organizations, up to certain limits defined by a percentage of the adjusted gross income, and to certain other organizations, also up to a specific percentage.
b. All state and local taxes paid (including sales taxes separately quoted by the vendor), with minor exceptions

*such as motor vehicle license fees, liquor and tobacco
taxes, and special assessments. No federal taxes are deductible as nonbusiness deductions.*
*c. Casualty and theft losses in excess of insurance com-
pensation.*
*d. Medical and dental expenses in excess of a certain
percentage of the adjusted gross income.*
e. Interest payments, with minor exceptions.
*f. Expenses (up to a specified point) for the care of chil-
dren in day-care centers.*
*g. Certain expenses related to employment, such as
union dues, and the expenses of certain tools, supplies,
special clothing, and professional journals.*

Instead of itemizing deductions, the taxpayer can claim a
zero bracket amount, formerly known as the standard deduction. Under the Revenue Act of 1978, this amount was increased from $2,200 to $2,300 for single taxpayers and heads
of households, from $3,200 to $3,400 for married couples,
and from $1,600 to $1,700 for married persons filing separate
returns.

Exemptions. For the taxable years through 1969, a taxpaying husband was allowed a $600 exemption for himself, for
his spouse, and for each dependent, as defined by law. Under
the provisions of the Tax Reform Act of 1969, the exemption
was changed to $625 in 1970, increasing to $750 in 1973, and
increased again to $1,000 by the Revenue Act of 1978.

To qualify as a dependent, a person has to receive more
than half of his support from the taxpayer (with special rules
when several persons provide joint support of a dependent).
The person must also receive less than $750 (in 1973 and after)
per year gross income (except for students and persons under
nineteen years of age) and be related, as defined, or living in
the taxpayer's home.

Tax Rates. The tax liability is determined by applying the
tax rates to the sum of the total income, or by using the tax
tables (in the case of incomes of $20,000 or less). Separate
rate tables are applicable to single persons, married taxpayers,
and unmarried heads of households, the latter receiving some
benefits from the income-splitting provisions.

The effective rate on the entire amount of a particular
taxable income is much lower than the "marginal rate,"
which rate applies only to the excess of income over the
previous bracket figure. The tax rates change frequently,

making it necessary to consult each year's current Internal Revenue Service instructions for the latest rates.

Withholding. With minor exceptions, all employers are required to withhold tax on a current basis from employees' paychecks and to transmit the sums to the government. Thus, when taxpayers file their returns at the end of the year, they merely pay the difference due or receive a refund if an overpayment has been made.

Withholding is not applied to other incomes. Persons not covered by withholding and those subject to withholding but earning in excess of a certain sum are required to file declarations of estimated income and to pay the tax on a quarterly basis during the year.

Capital Gains and Losses. Capital gains from the sale of property held more than six months are taxable at a special lower rate. Gains on property held less than six months are taxable at regular rates.

Special provisions are made for owner-occupied residences, which in effect exempt the gain from the sale of a home if one of the same or of greater value is purchased or built within a given time interval. There are special provisions, also, relating to the sale or exchange of owner-occupied residences by persons age 65 or older. Capital losses may be deducted only from capital gains or from other income in limited amounts.

Minimum Tax. Prior to the Revenue Act of 1978, a 15% minimum tax was imposed on "preference income." This was defined to include items such as long-term capital gains, the excess of accelerated depreciation over straight-line depreciation on real property, and the compensation element in exercised stock options, to the extent such income exceeds a certain sum plus the income tax otherwise payable. For a long time, however, tax reform advocates had contended that the minimum tax was inadequate when tax shelters permitted a taxpayer to avoid paying any tax whatsoever on the half of capital gains subject to ordinary tax.

In response to this criticism, the 1978 legislation included a new, alternative minimum tax calculated on the sum of taxable income, capital gains, and excess itemized deductions, less a $20,000 exemption. It is payable when it exceeds regular tax liability plus the 15% minimum tax.

Corporate Income Tax. The corporate income tax applies to the net profit of corporations, calculated in the usual accounting manner, apart from a large number of special rules relating to such items as depreciation, depletion, and research and development expenses. Bond interest is fully deductible.

Contributions to charity are deductible up to a low percentage of the net income. As with the personal income tax, losses incurred in one year may be carried back three years and forward five years against the earnings of those years.

Administration. The tax is administered by the Internal Revenue Service. Returns are filed with the district offices of the service. All returns are subject to a routine office audit. Larger returns, in addition to all those about which there is any doubt, receive more thorough field audits. Except in cases of fraud, the examination of returns is subject to a three-year statute of limitations.

General regulations are issued by the Internal Revenue Service to amplify the code. Rulings are issued on specific cases as they arise and are summarized in the semimonthly *Internal Revenue Bulletin.* Appeals from the rulings may be taken by the taxpayer to a Tax Court or, in some instances, to a federal district court.

State Income Taxes. State rates are low by comparison with the federal rates. Progression in rates is usually limited and ends at a low figure. Business and personal deductions are similar to those of the federal tax, but exemptions are higher. Some of the taxes apply only to income of residents of the state, but others apply only to income earned in the state, regardless of residence.

Most states, however, combine the tax bases, taxing residents on all income and nonresidents on the income earned in the state. The amount of double taxation is lessened, however, by reciprocal provisions in the laws of most states. Most of the states also impose corporate income taxes. The rates range from 1% to about 10%, with limited progression in a few instances.

Economic Aspects

The role of the income tax in the tax structure and the effects it has on the economy have become questions of major significance as the tax has grown in importance. A number of arguments have been advanced in support of taxation as it exists in the United States. The tax raises revenue in a way that conforms to one's ability to pay; it can be adjusted to reflect the special circumstances of the taxpayer, such as the number of dependents, medical expenses, and other factors; it can be used as a tool for lessening the inequality of income distribution in the country; and it produces a high revenue yield.

On the other hand, the income tax has been attacked sharply from many quarters. Some argue that the progressive nature of the tax is bad, since it weakens a person's incentive to work, to develop and expand a business, and to invest. The administration of the tax laws is a massive task; evasion and dishonesty are ever-present problems. The laws often impose double taxation, as in the case of corporate earnings and savings. They penalize persons who have not yet accumulated wealth, in comparison with those who have. Finally, the tax code is such a massive document and is so riddled with provisions favoring various special interest groups that it actually imposes a far more inequitable tax than would appear on the surface.

If a particular income tax is to meet the threefold requirements of equity, neutrality, and administrative feasibility, certain problems must be solved in the establishment of the tax. An accurate definition of the word *income* must be used. Increases in the value of assets, known as capital gains, must be treated satisfactorily. If certain types of income are to be excluded from the taxable income to avoid inequities or to minimize administrative problems, they must be defined with care. If the tax is to rest upon net income, provision must be made for the deduction of those expenses involved in gaining the income, generally known as business expenses. Some principled line between business and personal expenses must be drawn. Rules must be established to control the allocation of income and expenditures to particular time periods.

It is probably desirable to have a system that would permit the adjustment of income in terms of certain elements that affect the standard of living within a given income—elements such as the number of dependents and extraordinary expenses. The taxpaying unit must be defined consistently and fairly.

From the standpoint of fiscal policy—that is, the attempt to gain greater economic stability by the adjustment of government revenues and expenditures—the income tax is widely believed to have an important advantage. Because of its exemptions and progressive rates, its yield tends to fall in recessions and rise more rapidly than the national income in inflationary periods. Thus, it cushions the fall of purchasing power in recessions and slows its increase in inflationary periods. This effect, however, proved counterproductive during

The Budget Dollar
Fiscal Year 1979 Estimate

Where It Comes From...

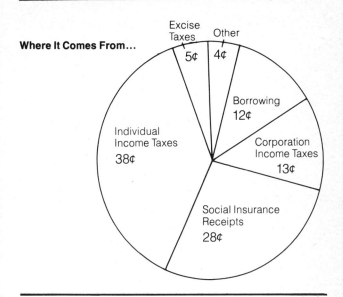

Excise Taxes 5¢

Other 4¢

Borrowing 12¢

Corporation Income Taxes 13¢

Individual Income Taxes 38¢

Social Insurance Receipts 28¢

Where It Goes...

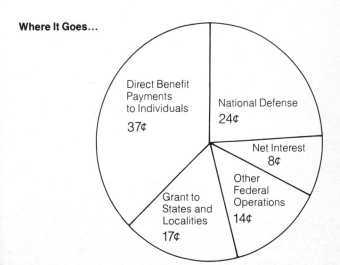

Direct Benefit Payments to Individuals 37¢

National Defense 24¢

Net Interest 8¢

Other Federal Operations 14¢

Grant to States and Localities 17¢

the recession of the mid-1970s, which was accompanied by rapid inflation.

If the rates are too high relative to the government's revenue needs at full employment, some economists believe that the tax can produce "fiscal drag," curtailing recovery before full employment is reached, as apparently occurred in the early 1960s. On the other hand, there is little visible evidence to support the view that the income tax's "built-in flexibility" has contributed significantly in moderating economic fluctuations or in curbing economic expansion. The fluctuating yield appears as a definite disadvantage to those who believe that the use of fiscal policy for economic stabilization is ineffectual. The federal tax is also a disadvantage to subordinate units of government, such as states and cities, which often have limited borrowing capacities and are not in a position to conduct deliberate fiscal policy. The income tax is often used as a well-concealed way of implementing various currently popular social policies, making it difficult for interested parties to respond and criticize the tax as their own interests dictate.

7.
Criminal Law

"Criminal law" is the body of law that defines criminal offenses, establishes the procedures for the apprehension, charging, and trial of suspected offenders, and fixes the penalties and methods of treatment applicable to convicted offenders. Every organized society has a body of rules, norms, or customs to protect the security of individuals and the survival of the group. The distinction between the criminal law and other forms of social control, however, is ordinarily not sharply drawn in primitive societies. Even in modern Anglo-American law the distinction between criminal law and "tort law" is hard to draw. For most purposes, it is enough to say that a tort is a private injury and that the purpose of a tort suit is primarily to obtain compensation from the wrongdoer for injuries sustained by the victim.

A crime, on the other hand, even though it may (and ordinarily does) involve injury to some individual, is conceived of as an offense against the state and is punishable as such. Thus the same conduct may render the wrongdoer liable in tort to compensate the victim for injuries inflicted and also answerable to the state in a criminal proceeding. Tort law and criminal law may also be distinguished by the procedures employed and the sanctions imposed.

Sources of Criminal Law

Although the criminal law of the United States clearly reveals its derivation from the English common law, the adoption of the common law was neither complete nor uniform in the American colonies. After the American Revolution the states incorporated into their law the English common law as it existed prior to a specified date (either 1607, when the settlement at Jamestown was founded, or 1776, the date of the Declaration of Independence). The English common law was made subject to the Constitution of the United States and to the state constitutions and was generally adopted only insofar as it was compatible with the conditions of the new nation. These limitations encouraged the rejection of certain archaic features of the common law of crimes, particularly those relating to outmoded and degrading forms of punishment.

In more than half of the states the common law of crimes

has been expressly or implicitly repealed by legislation. The effect of such enactments is primarily that no person may be tried for any offense that is not specified in the statutory law of the state. Common-law principles retain great influence in such jurisdictions, however, because the state statutes on crime often are simply codifications of the common law, and their terms and provisions are ordinarily interpreted by reference to the common law. No federal offenses other than those provided for by statute are recognized. But, again, federal criminal statutes are interpreted in the light of the common law.

In the states in which the common law of crimes has not been repealed, prosecutions for common-law offenses not specified in the statutes are possible and sometimes occur. Examples of the most numerous of these prosecutions are those for conspiracy, criminal solicitation, and breach of peace.

A great many criminal laws have been passed in the United States since the first quarter of the nineteenth century. It has been estimated that the number of offenses defined by legislatures doubled in the first half of the twentieth century. But this frequent resort to penal, or criminal, legislation has not ordinarily been accompanied by a careful consideration of the issues of penal regulation by U.S. lawmakers. In many states the so-called penal, or criminal, codes are simply collections of individual provisions enacted at different times in response to particular problems that were then current. There was little effort to relate the parts to the whole or to define or promote any general theory of social control through penal measures. As a result, U.S. criminal legislation characteristically is poorly drafted, inconsistent, and ill-considered. And the courts have not succeeded in making sense of U.S. criminal law through the processes of judicial interpretation.

Throughout the United States in the twentieth century a more serious interest in criminal law has developed. By the beginning of the 1970s, criminal code revision was being undertaken by the federal government and many states, including heavily populated states like California, Michigan, and Texas. This interest has been significantly stimulated by the American Law Institute, a private organization of lawyers and judges, which began the drafting of a model penal code in 1952. The model code represents the cooperative efforts of judges, lawyers, legal scholars, and behavioral scientists. In 1930 the American Law Institute published a model code of criminal procedure. The adoption of the Federal Rules of Criminal Procedure in 1946 also provided a stimulus for procedural reform in other jurisdictions.

Substantive Criminal Law

The substantive criminal law is concerned with defining the kinds of conduct that are to be considered criminal, thereby making the perpetrators eligible for punishment. *Conduct*, as the word is used in this context, should be understood as covering not only specified acts or omissions but also accompanying mental states as well. The substantive law consists of more than statutes or judicial decisions that define particular offenses. Certain doctrines—some of constitutional origin—also exclude various kinds of conduct from the definition of criminal behavior. Similarly, certain principles apply to all or to large parts of the substantive law and qualify criminal legislation even though the principles are not expressed in the particular statute defining the offense.

Limitations on the definition of criminal conduct include the following:

1. *Constitutional Limitations*—The criminal law, having at its disposal some of the most rigorous sanctions within the power of the state, inevitably poses basic problems regarding the relations of the individual and the state. It is not surprising, therefore, that the regulation of the criminal process is one of the chief objectives of U.S. constitutional law. Most of the constitutional limitations apply to matters of criminal procedure, but others directly limit the power of legislatures and courts to condemn certain types of behavior as "criminal."

No political entity may denounce and punish behavior that falls outside its jurisdiction. Thus the federal government, being a government of delegated powers, may declare as criminal only behavior that falls within the scope of its granted authority. The validity of a federal criminal statute must be predicated on bases of authority such as the power of Congress to regulate foreign and interstate commerce, the federal government's revenue and war powers, and powers relating to the currency. The individual state also is presumably limited to the punishment of behavior that occurs within its geographical boundaries or, if it has occurred elsewhere, to any conduct that affects the interests of the state in some substantial way.

The constitutional grant of freedom of speech and religion

makes conduct that falls within these provisions immune from criminal punishment by federal or state authority. Thus, in *Cantwell* v. *Connecticut* (1940), the U.S. Supreme Court overturned a state conviction for the common-law crime of breach of peace, finding that the defendant's conduct was within his protected freedom of religion. In the U.S. political system the states enjoy broad powers of regulation, including regulation by criminal sanctions, in public health, safety, and morals. Occasionally, however, attempts at such "police power" regulation have been held to exceed the limits of constitutional tolerance. In a recent example, the Supreme Court struck down a zoning ordinance of the city of East Cleveland, Ohio, that made it a crime for a grandmother to allow two of her grandsons, who were cousins, to live in her home (*Moore* v. *East Cleveland*, 1977). State criminal legislation may be voided when the state has attempted to enter a field that is validly regulated by the federal government if the state statute is deemed incompatible with the proper exercise of federal power. The equal-protection clause of the Fourteenth Amendment forbids the enactment of criminal legislation that discriminates on grounds of race or color or that creates other unreasonable classifications.

Various other constitutional provisions have been employed to limit legislative powers in defining criminal offenses. In *Robinson* v. *California* (1962), the U.S. Supreme Court resorted to the constitutional provisions that forbid "cruel and unusual punishment" in order to invalidate a state statute that imposed criminal sanctions on persons addicted to narcotic drugs. The same clause has also been used to strike down mandatory death sentences (*Woodson* v. *North Carolina*, 1976).

2. **Legality**—The first article of the U.S. Constitution (Sec. 9, cl. 3, and Sec. 10, cl. 1) and the constitutions of most of the states contain provisions prohibiting the enactment of ex post facto ("after the fact") legislation. These provisions represent an expression in constitutional form of one aspect of the broad principle of the rule of law in the criminal process.

The rule of law, or principle of legality, has been employed in four senses. The first and most common sense is that there can be no crime without a criminal law. Conduct may be immoral or antisocial, but it is not criminal unless there is a law that forbids it. Second, the principle directs that only legally prescribed punishment can be imposed upon a convicted person. In the United States it has been held that the principle is not violated by statutes that provide sentences without a specified duration, so long as the maximum sentence is prescribed. Third, the principle of legality forbids retroactive penal legislation (penal laws passed after the deed is done). In order that a person may be convicted, a law must have been in effect at the time of the conduct, forbidding the conduct and rendering it punishable. It is this aspect of the principle to which the ex post facto clause of the U.S. Constitution directly relates. Fourth, the principle of legality requires that criminal statutes be interpreted strictly—ambiguities and vagueness must be resolved in favor of the accused. If a criminal statute is vague, so that a person cannot tell what conduct is criminal by reading the statute, the law is unconstitutional as a violation of due process. The rule of strict construction may not be used, however, to defeat the clear purposes of the legislature.

All of the applications of the principle of legality are intended to ensure that no person will be punished as a criminal except on the basis of definite law existing at the time the act in question was committed. The major attack on the principle has been made by some criminologists and psychiatrists who contend that the fixing of maximum sentences handicaps both the rehabilitation of the criminal and the defense of social interests. Despite these arguments, it is widely accepted that, although considerable discretion should be allowed for the individualized treatment of offenders, power in a democratic community must be subjected to reasonable restraints.

3. **Entrapment**—The scope of criminal liability is limited by the doctrine of entrapment. This doctrine declares that, when acts that would otherwise be considered criminal are committed by an accused person as a result of the activity of law-enforcement officers who implant a criminal intent in the accused's mind and directly instigate the acts, criminal liability does not attach. Frequently, however, the prosecution may defeat an entrapment defense by showing that the accused was predisposed to commit the crime.

Entrapment should be distinguished from situations in which an officer does not instigate the offense but merely provides the opportunity or occasion for its commission. The distinction in many cases, not surprisingly, is a difficult one to draw. The doctrine of entrapment has received its most frequent application in such cases as liquor violations and gambling and narcotics offenses. Its application to cases of homicide and those involving serious bodily injury is far from clear. Dispute has also arisen regarding the precise theoretical basis for the doctrine. By far the majority of courts take the view that an accused who is led into conduct otherwise criminal by the "creative activity" of law-enforcement officers has committed no offense. Some authorities have urged that under such circumstances an offense has been committed but that the state should withhold punishment from the offender. However it is articulated, the doctrine reflects ethical repugnance to such law-enforcement measures.

General Doctrines and Principles.

The substantive criminal law contains a number of general doctrines and principles that form an important part of the definition of criminal behavior, even though they customarily are not expressed in statutes that define particular offenses. In a fully articulated penal code these matters are dealt with in the general part of the code:

1. *Criminal Act or Omission*—It is generally agreed that an essential ingredient of any crime is a voluntary act or omission. An act may be defined as a willed muscular contraction. Movements performed in a state of "open-eyed consciousness" are acts, even though the acts are the product of a mental disorder. In such cases, exculpation (being cleared from blame) must come, if at all, by virtue of the insanity defense. Criminal liability may also be brought about by a failure to act when the accused was under a legal duty to act and was reasonably capable of doing so. The duty to act, however, is defined rather narrowly in the Anglo-American law. There is thus no general obligation to protect others from harm. These restrictions on the principle have often been attacked, but proposals for the drastic enlargement of the legal duty to act have generally been rejected.

2. *Mens Rea or Mental Element*—In general, the definition of an offense includes not only an act or omission and its consequences but also the accompanying mental state of the actor. An appraisal of the moral character or social dangerousness of the offender requires that it be known whether the conduct was purposeful, reckless, negligent, or accidental. Frequently, in the modern era, the criminal law has imposed liability on the accused without requiring the showing of a guilty mind. Nevertheless, the tradition of the common law strongly supports the belief that the stigma of serious criminality ought not, on grounds of justice or utility, to be imposed on a person who produces harm inadvertently or

accidentally. "Even a dog," wrote Justice Oliver Wendell Holmes, "distinguishes between being stumbled over and being kicked."

3. *Absolute Liability*—Since the eighteenth century a considerable body of penal law has developed in which no intent or other mental state need be shown. The absence of the requirement of mens rea, or harmful state of mind, characterizes a few offenses such as statutory rape, in which knowledge that the girl is below the age of consent is not necessary for liability. Another such crime is bigamy, which in most jurisdictions may be committed even though the parties believe in complete good faith that they are free to marry. For the most part, however, absolute liability (in which the state of mind is irrelevant) operates in offenses to which only slight or moderate penalties are attached. These offenses, sometimes called "public welfare offenses," are most commonly concerned with economic regulations or with protecting public health and safety. In addition, for most so-called crimes of absolute liability, the requirement of proving a certain mental state is abolished only for certain elements of the crime.

4. *Ignorance and Mistake*—When the accused is operating under an assumption of fact which, although mistaken, is inconsistent with the mens rea that must be shown, no crime is committed. Thus one who takes and carries away the goods of another, believing them to be his own, does not commit larceny, for he lacks the intent to steal. If the offense is one of absolute liability, a mistake of fact about a material element of the offense does not relieve the actor of liability. Anglo-American law adheres to the maxim "ignorance of the law excuses no one." In general, therefore, it is no defense that the actor was unaware that his conduct was criminal.

5. *Responsibility*—It is universally recognized that, in appropriate cases, persons suffering from serious mental disorders should be relieved of the criminal consequences of their conduct. This principle has been part of the English common law for at least seven centuries. Nevertheless, sharp and persistent differences of opinion have been expressed regarding the proper legal test for responsibility.

The classic test, termed the "McNaghten test" after the case in which it was originally articulated, requires proof that at the time of the criminal act the accused had such a defect of reason, from disease of the mind, that he did not know the nature and quality of the act he was doing or that, if he did know it, he did not know that the act was wrong. Some courts have supplemented this rule by the "irresistible impulse" test, relieving the accused of criminal responsibility if he could not control his behavior because of mental disorder. A third alternative is the "Durham test," again named after a court decision, which states that an accused is not criminally responsible if his unlawful act was the product of mental disease or mental defect. Finally, the American Law Institute's model penal code provides a defense to a criminal charge when at the time of the act the accused, by reason of mental disorder or defect, lacked "substantial capacity to appreciate the criminality of his conduct or to conform his conduct to the requirements of law."

A successful insanity defense results in a verdict of "not guilty by reason of insanity" in most jurisdictions. But the defendant normally does not go free after such a verdict. Instead, he is usually committed to a mental hospital for treatment for as long a period as is deemed necessary—potentially for life.

Even when the accused's mental disorder is not so advanced as to result in irresponsibility, it may nevertheless affect the extent of criminal liability. Some U.S. courts have permitted the accused to show that his mental condition rendered him incapable of forming the mens rea required for a more serious offense, thereby reducing the seriousness of the offense for which he is convicted. Thus, if the defendant is able to demonstrate that he was incapable of premeditating, his offense may be reduced from first-degree murder to second-degree murder.

6. *Infancy*—Another aspect of criminal incapacity is that recognized in children. Under the common law no child below the age of seven was regarded as possessing criminal responsibility. A presumption of criminal incapacity applied to children from seven to fourteen years of age. The presumption could be overcome by showing that the child understood the nature and consequences of his conduct. In most states of the United States the minimum age of capacity has been raised by statute. The criminal capacity of children has been further modified by the widespread enactment of juvenile court laws.

7. *Intoxication*—The Anglo-American law takes an ambivalent and unsatisfactory position on the significance of intoxication to criminal liability. It is commonly said that intoxication is no defense to a criminal charge. The statement, however, does not mean that drunkenness has no significance

in determining the existence or the degree of criminal liability. Drunkenness may affect the capacity of the accused to form the mens rea required for the commission of the offense. When this applies, the accused may escape liability or be found guilty of a less serious offense. Thus, a person so inebriated that he lacks the capacity to form an intent to steal is not guilty of larceny even though he takes and carries away the goods of another.

8. *Vicarious Liability*—The common law of crimes ordinarily proceeds on the assumption that "guilt is personal." Thus, in general, a person may be held criminally accountable for the conduct of another only when he in some way participated in or contributed to the conduct. During the nineteenth and twentieth centuries, however, legislatures created numerous statutory offenses in which the basis of liability is the existence of an "employment" relationship between the accused and the person engaging in the criminal act.

The criminal responsibility of corporate bodies and of private associations such as partnerships and labor unions constitutes another type of vicarious criminal responsibility. Ordinarily a corporation is held criminally liable for the act of an officer or employee, but a fine levied on the corporate body involves loss to the stockholders, who, in most instances, did not participate in the criminal act and were unaware of its occurrence. Nevertheless, the stockholders do not suffer the stigma of personal conviction, and their loss is limited to the amount of their investment in the corporation.

9. *Parties to Crime*—A person may be held legally accountable for the conduct of another through the doctrines of "accessoryship," that is, that one person is an accessory to the crime of another. The common law drew elaborate distinctions among the various participants in a crime based on their presence, the directness of their aid, and the timing of their aid (whether it was given before or after the crime was committed). The clear tendency of the modern U.S. law is to eliminate the common-law distinctions between accessories to a crime and principal offenders and to treat all participants in a crime as principals. "Accessories after the fact," however, are still punished only for concealing or obstructing the apprehension of known fugitives from justice.

10. *Consent to Crime and Condoning Crime*—The proposition sometimes expressed that "the consent of the victim to the criminal conduct of the accused is no defense" needs to be qualified. In cases of homicide, dueling, and other

instances of serious bodily injury, the consent of the victim does *not* excuse the criminal behavior. On the other hand, in a considerable number of serious offenses, the lack of consent of the victim is defined to be an indispensable element of the crime. Thus, in forcible rape the intercourse must occur against the will of the victim. Larceny requires the taking of goods from the possession of the owner without his consent. Except in a few statutory offenses, the accused is not relieved of the liability for a completed crime by the fact that the victim subsequently condones the accused's conduct.

11. **Necessity and Coercion**—The doctrines of necessity relate to situations in which a person, confronted by the overwhelming pressure of natural forces, must make a choice between evils and chooses to engage in conduct, otherwise criminal, as the lesser of the evils. The defense of duress, or coercion, relates to situations in which the accused acted under threats of imminent death or serious bodily injury by third parties. This defense may not be used when the accused has killed an innocent victim in order to save his own life.

12. **Self-Defense and Justification**—The Anglo-American law recognizes a number of particular situations in which the use of force, even deadly force, is excused or justified. The most important body of law in this area relates to self-defense. In most U.S. jurisdictions deadly force may be employed whenever one reasonably believes that he is placed in the imminent peril of death or serious bodily injury by the conduct of another and believes also that the killing of the other is necessary to save his own life.Thus, justification may be granted when the killing was, in fact, not necessary, as long as the actor reasonably believed it to be so. On the other hand, an actual belief is not sufficient if it is found to have been unreasonable under the circumstances. A few U.S. jurisdictions hold that belief, even unreasonable belief, excuses the actor; and the American Law Institute's model penal code asserts that this is the preferable view. The federal courts and probably a majority of state courts permit the defendant to stand his ground and to kill when the requirements of self-defense are met.

The law of justification provides varying requirements for the use of force in other situations. These include the use of force to protect third parties from harm, to prevent the commission of a felony, to arrest a fleeing felon, and to defend property or a habitation from the aggressions of another.

Particular Offenses

Certain types of behavior are universally recognized as being dangerous to the security of individual and social interests. All advanced legal systems condemn as criminal such conduct as treason, murder, aggravated assault, theft, robbery, burglary, arson, and rape. In contrast, substantial differences in the definition of minor criminal behavior occur among jurisdictions:

1. *Classification of Offenses*—Under the common law offenses were classified into three principal categories: treason, felony, and misdemeanor. Significant differences in the penalties imposed and the criminal procedures employed resulted from this division. U.S. jurisdictions generally distinguish between felonies and misdemeanors. Although the definition of felony is not uniform in the states, it is typically defined as a crime punishable by a term of imprisonment of not less than one year in a state penitentiary. Misdemeanors are often defined as offenses punishable only by fines or by terms of imprisonment in county or local jails.

The distinction between a felony and a misdemeanor is less significant for modern law, and many commentators have questioned its utility. Certain consequences, however, continue to result from the distinction. Thus, a convicted felon may suffer the loss of civil rights, which are retained by a misdemeanant (a person convicted of a misdemeanor). Certain substantive doctrines take the distinction into account, for example, the authorization of the use of deadly force to effect the arrest of a felon but not of a misdemeanant. In addition to felonies and misdemeanors, U.S. jurisdictions recognize a class of minor offenses that may be described as "quasi-crimes." Such offenses are typically created by a municipal ordinance or by a county authority. The penalties are comparatively trivial. Often the right to a jury trial is held not to extend to quasi-criminal proceedings, and the prosecution may not be required to establish guilt beyond a reasonable doubt.

Other classifications of crimes have been employed for various analytical purposes. In the survey that follows some of the major types of offenses are included in a classification of inchoate (preliminary) crimes, crimes against persons, crimes against property, and crimes against government.

2. *Preliminary Crimes*—The Anglo-American law defines

several offenses that are sometimes labeled "inchoate," or "preliminary," crimes, for which a person may be found guilty even though the criminal purpose may not have been achieved. The first of these is an offense, usually a misdemeanor, known most commonly in the United States as solicitation. The offense consists of urging or requesting another to commit a crime. The law states that to be classified as "inchoate," the crime solicited must be either a felony or a misdemeanor involving a breach of the peace. The crime of solicitation is complete when the solicitation is made; the solicitor's liability does not depend upon whether or not the other person commits the requested offense. Criminal legislation may also prohibit certain specified types of solicitation, such as a bribe, solicitation for immoral purposes, or inciting members of the armed forces to mutiny.

Criminal attempts constitute a second and more important category of inchoate offenses. "Attempt" consists of conduct intended to accomplish a criminal result that fails to be completed but that goes beyond the acts of preparation to a point dangerously close to the completion of the intended harm. The line between an act of mere preparation and an attempt is difficult to draw in many cases. Criminal attempt is said to require a specific intent to commit a particular crime rather than only a general criminal intent. Thus, although in certain situations murder may be committed even if there is no intent to kill, attempted murder cannot be established without proof of such intent. No defense is granted in the United States to an offender who voluntarily desists from committing the intended harm after his conduct has reached a point beyond mere preparation.

Conspiracy is defined by the common law as an agreement between two or more persons to accomplish an unlawful objective or to achieve a lawful end by the use of unlawful means. To this definition, American jurisdictions generally add the requirement that one of the parties to the agreement must commit an overt act designed to advance the purposes of the conspiracy. In the absence of statutory provisions to the contrary, the unlawful objective need not be one that would be criminal if achieved by an individual acting alone. Thus, agreements to attain noncriminal ends that were conceived by the courts to be immoral or oppressive have been punished. The control of criminal activity involving group action is a problem of serious proportions in all advanced societies. The Anglo-American law of conspiracy, however, is far from satisfactory in that it does not clearly define all of the crucial elements of the offense. The procedures and rules of evidence that are applied in conspiracy prosecutions often place the defense at a serious disadvantage. In the breadth of its scope and the amorphous nature of its definitions, the offense of conspiracy has a unique position in the Anglo-American law.

3. **Crimes Against Persons**—In any advanced system of criminal justice, minimizing the crimes of violence is a matter of first concern to the legal order. The most serious of these crimes, of course, are criminal homicides. Murder as defined in the Anglo-American system may be described as the killing of another human being with malice aforethought. The phrase *malice aforethought* has a technical significance and, in the course of time, has acquired meanings quite different from those commonly understood. Thus, a killing may be said to be with malice aforethought when the accused intended to kill either the victim or another person, intended to inflict serious bodily harm on the victim, did not intend to kill but engaged in extremely reckless conduct, killed a person in the course of committing some other felony, or killed a peace officer while resisting a lawful arrest. All of these categories are subject to important qualifications and refinements. Most U.S. states have divided the crime of murder into degrees, reserving capital punishment or the most stringent penalties for murder in the first degree. First-degree murder is variously defined but ordinarily includes premeditated and deliberate killings and often killings that occurred in the course of committing certain violent felonies. There are also second- and, sometimes, third-degree murders defined by each state.

Several lesser homicide offenses exist. Involuntary manslaugher ordinarily involves a killing caused by the reckless or grossly negligent conduct of the offender or a homicide resulting from commission of an unlawful act other than a felony. Voluntary manslaughter is ordinarily a killing in the "heat of passion" by an accused who acted in response to provocation by the victim. The provocation must be of a sufficiently serious nature to justify reducing the offense from murder to manslaughter. Many states recognize a lesser offense, sometimes called reckless homicide, chiefly involving deaths resulting from automobile accidents.

In addition to the criminal homicides, the law defines other offenses against persons. Two of these, forcible rape and kidnapping, are often punished as severely as are some homicides. Various sorts of assault and battery are punished in all of the states. Under common law, the offense of mayhem was committed when the accused cut off or otherwise deprived another of the use of a limb or a body member, thereby impairing the ability of the victim to defend himself. The crime of mayhem, usually broadened to include other kinds of serious bodily harm, has been made part of the statutory law of many U.S. jurisdictions.

4. *Crimes Against Property*—Theft is the major crime against property. The basic theft offense in the common law was larceny, which consisted of the taking and carrying away of goods from the possession of another without the person's consent. In order for the action to be considered a larceny, the offender must have an intent to steal, defined as an intent to deprive the owner of his goods permanently. Embezzlement is another theft offense. In general, it is the misappropriation of the goods of another that have been delivered to or entrusted to the possession of the offender. Thus, the difference between larceny and embezzlement lies in whether the offender's initial possession of the goods was lawful or not. A third important category of theft is the crime of false pretenses. This offense ordinarily consists of inducing another to part with the ownership of goods by false representations. Akin to false pretenses is the offense of obtaining credit by fraud. Finally, the law punishes the offense of receiving stolen goods by one who knows or believes them to be stolen and intends to deprive the owner permanently of the property. Since the one who receives the stolen goods provides the market for them, the prevention of such conduct is obviously crucial if large-scale thefts are to be discouraged. Because the line between the various categories of theft is often difficult to draw, a number of U.S. jurisdictions have enacted "consolidated theft laws" that define a single statutory offense containing the elements of all the major theft crimes; these laws permit convictions if it is shown that the offender's conduct falls within any of these categories.

In addition to the major categories of theft, legislatures have enacted a wide range of statutes concerning offenses relating to various aspects of modern commercial enterprise. Typical of these statutes are those designed to eliminate frauds and to force full disclosures in the sale and issuance of corporate securities.

The law also defines as criminal various types of conduct that constitute threats to both bodily security and property.

Arson is defined under common law as the malicious burning of the property of another. Under modern law the definition has been expanded to include the voluntary burning of one's own dwelling.

The most important offenses of this kind are robbery, burglary, and arson. Robbery may be regarded as aggravated larceny; it consists of taking property from the person or presence of another by placing him in fear. The statutes usually authorize greater penalties if robbery is accomplished by the use of a firearm or other dangerous weapon. Burglary under the common law was the breaking and entering of the dwelling house of another at night with the intent to commit a felony in the structure. In modern statutory law the offense of burglary has frequently been expanded to include buildings other than houses and times other than night. Arson under the common law consisted of the malicious burning of the dwelling house of another. Modern law has, again, broadened the offense to encompass the burning of other structures, including one's own dwelling. Widespread insurance coverage is probably an important reason for the change.

5. *Crimes Against Government*—In the feudal system the most heinous offense was the breach of the allegiance owed by the vassal to his lord. In the modern era offenses that threaten the security of the state are treated with exceptional seriousness. Treason is the only offense defined in the United States Constitution and "consist[s] only in levying War against [the United States], or in adhering to their enemies, giving them aid and comfort" (Art. III, Sec. 3). The same constitutional provision limits the penalties and regulates the modes of proof in treason prosecutions. Besides treason, a wide range of lesser "political crimes" has been defined, such as theft of military and governmental secrets. In another important category of offenses are those that may be described as crimes against public justice and governmental processes. These include such offenses as bribing public officials, committing perjury, exerting improper influence on members of juries, and altering or destroying public records. Some of this conduct is not only made punishable by the criminal law but is also subject to the contempt powers of the courts.

Criminal Procedure

The law of criminal procedure regulates the mode of apprehending, charging, and trying suspected offenders, the imposition of penalties on convicted offenders, and the methods of challenging the legality of convictions after judgments are made. The law in this area is called upon to advance and reconcile interests of the greatest importance. It must contribute effectively to the attainment of public peace and good order. At the same time it must afford realistic protection for the rights of persons against whom the criminal justice system proceeds.

1. **Constitutional Limitations**—The regulation of criminal procedure is one of the primary concerns of U.S. constitutional law. Certain protections against oppressive procedures, many of which derive from English common law and constitutional history, are explicitly recognized in the Bill of Rights.

Thus the Fourth Amendment prohibits unreasonable searches and seizures; the Fifth Amendment requires the use of an indictment or presentment in cases of infamous crime, prohibits double jeopardy (being tried twice for the same offense), and states the general requirement of due process of law. The Sixth Amendment guarantees a speedy and public trial in criminal cases, the right of trial by jury and the rights to be confronted by hostile witnesses, to have a compulsory process in order to obtain favorable witnesses, and to be tried in the district in which the crime was committed. The Eighth Amendment forbids excessive bail and cruel and unusual punishments. Most of the specific restraints of the Bill of Rights are made applicable to the states through the due process clause of the Fourteenth Amendment. In addition, the constitutions of the states contain provisions that regulate criminal procedure. Some of these protections are expressed in language identical or similar to the Bill of Rights.

2. **Jurisdiction and Venue**—Although the criminal jurisdiction of state and federal courts is subject to constitutional

An alleged criminal appears before the court at a pre-trial hearing in Florida. The Sixth Amendment guarantees a speedy, public trial and the right to trial by jury in criminal cases.

limitations, the rules of jurisdiction applied in most states are derived from the common law. In some respects they are more restrictive than might be permitted under constitutional authority. The jurisdiction of a court refers to its capacity to take valid legal action. Questions of jurisdiction may relate to the subject matter of the prosecution, the geographical limits of the court's power, or the question of whether the defendant is properly before the court. Thus, in most states minor offenses may be tried before a magistrate or justice of the peace. These tribunals lack jurisdiction to try more serious crimes. Such trials must be held in courts of general criminal jurisdiction.

In the United States a court's jurisdiction over criminal conduct is primarily limited to conduct that occurred within the territorial limits of the particular state. In some instances state legislatures have extended jurisdiction to conduct occurring outside the state, if it directly affects the interests of the state or its citizens. The territorial principle has been similarly expanded in the federal courts. Finally, it is generally assumed that, except in the trial of petty offenses, the presence of the defendant before the court is essential to the court's jurisdiction. In many states, however, once the jurisdiction has been determined, it may not be defeated even if the defendant decides voluntarily not to appear in court. Rule 43 of the Federal Rules of Criminal Procedure provides that the voluntary absence of the defendant does not defeat continuation of the trial "in prosecutions of offenses not punishable by death."

Even if a court has jurisdiction over the subject matter of the prosecution and over the offender, the question of the proper place, or venue, of the trial remains. Constitutional provisions, such as that in the Sixth Amendment, as a rule provide that the defendant shall be tried in the district or county in which the crime occurred. This right may be waived by the defendant. Indeed, the accused may request a change of venue because of prejudice against him in the community or in the court.

3. *Arrest and Search*—The Fourth Amendment to the U.S. Constitution and similar provisions of state laws prohibit unreasonable searches and seizures. Since an arrest consists of the seizure of a person, the definition of *valid arrest* is subject to constitutional limitations. The constitutional criteria are held to be satisfied, however, by the common-law rules relating to arrest. In common law, an arrest may be made by a

The Fourth Amendment prohibits unreasonable searches and seizures. Evidence obtained in a search after an illegal arrest may be inadmissible in a criminal trial.

warrant issued by a magistrate on the basis of evidence creating a reasonable belief that the person has committed an offense. In some cases, usually those involving a reasonable belief that the suspect has committed a felony, arrest may be made without a warrant. Modern legislation has often broadened arrest powers, particularly those of peace officers in misdemeanor cases. The constitutional validity of these statutes has ordinarily been upheld.

There are several legal consequences of illegal arrests. First of all, the arresting party may be held liable in a civil suit for damages. Second, since the use of force in making an arrest is usually justified only if the arrest is valid, the arresting party may be held criminally liable for any injuries that are inflicted upon the person he seeks to arrest. Another consequence is that any evidence obtained in a search after an illegal arrest may be rendered inadmissible in the criminal trial. This is the result of the "exclusionary rule," first recognized by the federal courts in 1911 and later (1961) held to be applicable to the states. The rule provides that evidence obtained by unreasonable searches and seizures is inadmissible in criminal trials. Although it has frequently been the subject of attack, many continue to feel that the rule offers the only realistic means of enforcing the Fourth Amendment's guarantees.

4. *Extradition*—The process by which a person charged with a crime in another jurisdiction is apprehended and returned to that jurisdiction is known as extradition. The procedures of extradition between sovereign nations are ordinarily regulated by treaty. The U.S. Constitution deals with similar problems among the various U.S. jurisdictions (Art. IV, Sec. 2, cl. 2). These provisions direct that fugitives from the justice of another state be given up on demand of that state. Because of problems in defining exactly who is a fugitive from justice, many states have adopted the Uniform Extradition Act, which eliminates the fugitive requirement. Somewhat similar provisions apply to transfer of persons charged with federal crimes from one federal district to another.

5. *Interrogation and Confessions*—A confession is a statement made out of court in which the accused acknowledges his guilt of an offense. In the later history of the common law a coerced, or involuntary, confession was not admissible in a criminal trial. The same is true under U.S. constitutional law. Some U.S. decisions regard the admission of an involuntary confession as a violation of the defendant's privilege against compulsory self-incrimination. But most decisions base their holdings on the requirements of the due process clauses. The scope of the confession rule has been the subject of sharp controversy. The view expressed most frequently in the older cases regards the confession as coerced only when the methods used to obtain it cast doubt on its accuracy or reliability. Beginning in the 1940s, however, the U.S. Supreme Court broadened the confession rule to invalidate not only those confessions that were probably unreliable but also those obtained by police methods that might be

regarded as reprehensible and improper. A voluntary confession is *competent* evidence of guilt, but in most U.S. jurisdictions it is not regarded as *sufficient* evidence of guilt. Thus, a confession must usually be corroborated by other evidence.

Without doubt, the most important and controversial effort of the Supreme Court to control police interrogation of criminal suspects before trial is represented by the so-called Miranda rule, named after the decision in *Miranda* v. *Arizona* (1966). Under this rule, a suspect must be warned of his right to remain silent and to have counsel present at the interrogation. If the right to counsel is not waived, the interrogation cannot properly proceed until the suspect's lawyer is present. If the person interrogated is financially unable to hire a lawyer, it is the obligation of the state to provide one when the questioning proceeds.

6. *Indictment and Information*—Criminal prosecutions begin with a formal accusation verified by an oath. Accusations are of three types: complaint, indictment, and information. A complaint is ordinarily made by a private citizen or police officer, and its use is confined principally to petty crimes. An indictment is a formal document returned by a grand jury. An information is an instrument prepared by the prosecutor. The Fifth Amendment to the Constitution requires an indictment in cases of capital or other infamous crimes in the federal courts. Rule 7 of the Federal Rules of Criminal Procedure, however, permits the prosecution of all but capital cases to begin by information if the accused waives an indictment by a grand jury. Waivers are frequent, and most prosecutions of even serious offenses in the federal courts are by information. During the nineteenth century many states abolished the grand jury and, subject to various regulations, authorized the use of information. The Supreme Court has held that such procedures do not violate the Fourteenth Amendment. Even in states that retain the grand jury, a provision is usually made in some cases to allow the accused to waive indictment.

An indictment or an information must sufficiently allege the relevant facts to establish the jurisdiction of the court in which the case is tried, provide the defendant with a notice of the charges against him so that he may prepare his defense, and protect the defendant from being tried again for the same offense. The failure of the indictment in any of these respects may subject it to a motion to quash (dismiss for legal insufficiency) by the defendant.

7. **Prosecution**—The function of prosecuting is performed mainly by public officials elected or appointed for this purpose. The office of public prosecutor (or state's attorney) emerged in the colonial period of American history. Today, the prosecutor exercises a wide discretion in the conduct of his office. He cannot be compelled to initiate a prosecution. In extreme cases in which a prosecutor fails to perform his duties, however, some states permit the appointment of special prosecutors to initiate and conduct proceedings in particular cases. On occasion, prosecutors guilty of the abuse of discretion have been removed from office. The rules of the states governing the dismissal of prosecutions by the prosecutor vary considerably. Such a motion, termed *nolle prosequi* ("to be unwilling to pursue"), requires the consent of the court in about half of the states. In the remaining states the prosecutor makes the final decision, and the court must grant the motion to dismiss. In practice, there is little difference between the two systems.

8. **Double Jeopardy**—The Fifth Amendment provides that no person shall "be subject for the same offense to be twice put in jeopardy of life or limb." Similar provisions are found in almost all state constitutions. In general, once jeopardy has "attached," an accused may not be tried again for the same offense, whatever the outcome of the first trial. Jeopardy is said to attach when the jury is sworn or—if the accused is tried without a jury—when the first witness is sworn. Certain exceptions to the general rule permit a second trial when the first proceeding is brought to a premature end by such circumstances as the illness or death of the trial judge or the failure of the jury to agree on a verdict. A second trial is also permitted if the accused himself requests the termination of the first trial. A new trial ordered by an appellate court when the criminal appeal was initiated by the convicted defendant does not constitute double jeopardy. In most circumstances, appeals by the government are not permitted.

The most difficult problems of double jeopardy involve the question of whether the second prosecution is for the "same" or for a "different" offense. Either acquittal or conviction prohibits a subsequent prosecution for a lesser included offense (for example, manslaughter is included in murder). In 1977 the Supreme Court decided that the reverse was also true and that a prosecution for the more serious offense after a conviction or acquittal of the included crime was barred by the double jeopardy clause.

The fact that offenses are defined in different sections of a statute does not prevent them from being regarded as the same offense for double jeopardy purposes. The test applied in the federal courts is that two offenses are different if each requires the proof of a fact that the other does not. Some of the state courts apply a broader test and hold that offenses are the same if they arise from the same "transaction." Thus, an offender who sells illegal narcotics that he has in his possession may not be convicted of both sale and possession. It has been held that if the same conduct constitutes a violation of state and federal law, the defender may be prosecuted by both jurisdictions. By the beginning of the 1960s, however, an increasing number of state laws prohibited state prosecutions after acquittals or convictions in the federal courts.

9. **Proof of Guilt and Fair Trial**—It is a basic principle of American law that the guilt of a criminal offense must be established beyond a reasonable doubt. The proposition does not require absolute certainty of guilt by the fact finder, but it does assume a higher order of proof than that normally required in civil proceedings—for example, proof showing that the disputed fact is more likely than not. Some states place the burden of proof to maintain certain defenses such as insanity on the defendant. With these exceptions, the prosecution's burden of proof beyond a reasonable doubt extends to all of the material elements of the crime. One of the material elements is the corpus delicti ("body of the crime"), which means simply that there must be proof that the crime was actually committed by someone. Other elements include identifying the defendant as the perpetrator and giving proof of criminal intent.

One of the central concerns of the administration of criminal justice is to provide the accused with a fair hearing on the issue of guilt and innocence. A number of constitutional provisions, notably the Sixth Amendment's provisions for a trial by jury, refer expressly to various aspects of a fair trial, a speedy and public trial, confrontation, and the compulsory process.

Since the 1930s the Supreme Court has considered a wide range of issues related to fair trials in the state courts. These concerns arise under the due process clause of the Fourteenth Amendment. Some of the most important Court decisions relate to the defendant's right to counsel. In the case of *Johnson* v. *Zerbst* (1938), the Sixth Amendment was interpreted as requiring courts to appoint lawyers in felony cases to represent defendants who lacked the means to employ counsel. The broad rule did not at first apply to criminal proceedings in the state courts. Instead, the due process clause of the Fourteenth Amendment was interpreted as requiring appointment of counsel for indigent defendants in state capital cases and in other cases only when it became necessary in order to ensure a fair trial. In the well-known case of *Gideon* v. *Wainwright* (1963), however, the Supreme Court imposed on the state courts obligations comparable to those that had been recognized in the federal courts for a generation. As a result, a defendant charged with any serious crime in a state court is entitled to have a lawyer appointed in his behalf if he is financially unable to hire one. At the same time the Court considerably expanded the rights to counsel of indigent persons who are seeking appeals in the state courts.

10. **Sentencing Practices**—Sentencing powers usually belong to the trial judge. Some jurisdictions authorize the jury to make recommendations to the court in capital cases, and under some statutes these recommendations are binding on the judge. In a few states juries have been granted additional sentencing powers and are required not only to return a verdict on the issue of guilt but also to specify the term of imprisonment to be imposed. Statutes on sentencing vary considerably. Some authorize only sentences for a definite term of years, but others provide for a term with stated maximum and minimum limits. In most states, parole boards are authorized to release prisoners under supervision before the expiration of the maximum periods of imprisonment. A presentence investigation by the probation service and a report to the trial judge are sometimes required before a sentence can be imposed or probation can be granted.

11. **Appellate Procedures**—After conviction, a defendant may move in the trial court to "arrest judgment," or he may file a legal application called a motion for a new trial. Among the grounds most frequently asserted in such motions are that the verdict is not supported by the law or the evidence, that newly discovered evidence has come to light, or that the court erred in its rulings on the admission of the evidence. In modern practice the legality of the conviction may also be challenged by a review in an appellate court. Under the common law, such criminal appeals were unknown.

Criminal appeals play an important role in the administration of justice in the United States. It was not until 1879, however, that writs of error in criminal cases were authorized in federal practice. Provisions for criminal appeals were made in many of the states at somewhat earlier dates. It has been held that the states are not under any constitutional obligation to provide review by the appellate courts in criminal cases, but if such appeals are authorized, they must be conducted fairly and without discrimination.

12. **Habeas Corpus**—Habeas corpus is an ancient common-law writ issued by a court or judge directing one who holds another person in his custody to bring that person (to "produce the body") for some specified purpose. Many varieties of the writ were recognized in common law. But the form of greatest importance, referred to by the English jurist Sir William Blackstone (1723–80) as "the great and efficacious writ," is habeas corpus ad subjiciendum ("you should have the body for submitting"), a writ used to correct violations of personal liberty through a judicial inquiry into the legality of a detention.

Although the use of habeas corpus has never been adequately traced in the colonial history of the United States, it is clear that the writ was adopted by many colonial courts as part of the common-law heritage. As early as 1692 South Carolina and Massachusetts enacted strong habeas corpus legislation. By the time the American Revolution began the right to habeas corpus was popularly regarded as among the basic protections of individual liberty. The U.S. Constitution provides that the privilege of the writ of habeas corpus "shall not be suspended, unless, when in Cases of Rebellion or Invasion the public Safety may require it" (Art. I, Sec. 9, cl. 2). The First American Congress enacted legislation that empowered justices of the Supreme Court and judges of district courts to grant the writ. It is generally agreed that the suspension of the writ requires the consent of Congress, but Congress can delegate the power to suspend the writ to the president. The state constitutions also contain provisions for the writ of habeas corpus and its suspension during periods of public emergency.

The writ of habeas corpus in state constitutional provisions ordinarily possesses the attributes of the common-law writ. Procedures for issuing the writ are regulated by legislation in most jurisdictions. Habeas corpus is conceived of as an extraordinary remedy and is usually not granted if other procedures are available. Thus, it is frequently said that a writ of habeas corpus cannot be used as a substitute for an appeal in a criminal case.

Since the enactment of the legislation of 1789, the habeas corpus jurisdiction of the federal courts has been expanded by a series of congressional acts. Of primary significance is the Act of 1867, which enlarged the habeas corpus jurisdiction to include cases of any person who is restrained "in violation of the Constitution, or of any treaty or law of the United States." These provisions, codified in 1874, survived without important change until 1948.

In 1948 Congress enacted a law authorizing a federal prisoner to attack his conviction in the court sentencing him on a variety of grounds, including lack of jurisdiction in the trial court and the denial of his constitutional rights. The filing of the motion for relief (the writ of habeas corpus) may be made at any time, but the court need not entertain successive motions for similar relief by the same prisoner. An application for habeas corpus must be denied when the prisoner has failed to utilize the statutory motion or when the motion has been denied, unless the statutory remedy appears to be inadequate to test the legality of the prisoner's detention. The validity of the statutory procedure has been upheld by the Supreme Court.

The habeas corpus jurisdiction of the federal courts over prisoners who have been convicted in state courts gives rise to even more difficult and delicate problems. Since 1867 the federal district courts have had jurisdiction over both federal and state prisoners who claim that their confinement is in violation of the Constitution or of federal law. Relief through federal habeas corpus is not available to the state prisoner until his court appeals within the state have been exhausted; this principle is expressed in a law enacted by Congress in 1948. The precise test of the requirement that state remedies must first be exhausted has been the source of judicial controversy, however, and other problems relating to the scope and availability of relief through federal habeas corpus have proved difficult. In the 1950s various legislative proposals, uniformly unsuccessful, were made for eliminating or drastically reducing federal habeas corpus jurisdiction over persons held under state laws. These proposals, nevertheless, often failed to take into account the substantial contributions to the quality of criminal justice in the states that have been made through the supervision of state procedures by the federal courts.

The writ of habeas corpus is recognized by the laws of the states as well as those of the federal government. A state court, however, may not issue the writ to release a person who is held under the authority of federal law. There is considerable diversity in the laws of the states as to the scope and function of the writ of habeas corpus and the procedures required to invoke it. For example, the writ may be strictly limited to attacks on the jurisdiction of the court in which the petitioner was convicted. In such states, other remedies may be available for use in asserting constitutional rights. Since World War II, many states have created statutory procedures to provide an efficient means for testing alleged deprivations of constitutional rights. Other states have adapted the writ of habeas corpus to accomplish this end.

The use of habeas corpus is by no means confined to challenges to the validity of criminal convictions on constitutional or other grounds. Frequently a writ may be requested on behalf of a person in police custody for the purpose of requiring the police either to charge the arrested person with an offense or to release him. Habeas corpus proceedings may be used to obtain the release of an accused person prior to trial on the ground that the bail is excessive. On occasion, relief through the use of a writ of habeas corpus has been granted to a prisoner who is unlawfully detained after the expiration of his sentence.

In the case of a person arrested on a warrant of extradition or of interstate surrender, habeas corpus may be used to challenge the validity of the warrant. The writ may also be employed in a wide variety of situations that do not involve criminal proceedings. Thus, competing claims to the custody of a minor may be adjudicated through a writ of habeas corpus. A person confined in a mental hospital may in some states bring about his release by showing at a habeas corpus hearing that he has recovered his sanity. The writ also has been employed to challenge the right of the military forces to retain persons in their custody. Nevertheless, the oldest use of the writ is still its most important use—to challenge the authority of the state to hold a person who claims that he is being unlawfully detained.

8.
Civil Rights and Civil Liberties

No other function of the Constitution or concern of the courts touches every person quite as deeply as civil rights and civil liberties. Next to the struggle for national independence, the struggle for civil liberties and for fundamental human freedoms has been one of the major features of modern American history. It has also been one of the most persistent and pervasive themes in literature, philosophy, and religious thought throughout history. President Franklin D. Roosevelt, for example, expressed all people's intense concern with civil liberties when, in his "Four Freedoms" address in 1941, he said that humanity looked forward to a world founded upon four essential freedoms: freedom of speech, freedom of religious worship, freedom from want, and freedom from fear. The first two have generally been thought of as basic civil liberties.

In justifying the American Revolution, therefore, the Declaration of Independence (1776) proclaimed the right of the people to abolish a government that failed to secure the people's "unalienable Rights," among which were "Life, Liberty, and the pursuit of Happiness." The Declaration, in effect, stated that the American colonists were seeking not only to throw off a foreign yoke but also to become a free people—a country that would enjoy self-rule and the inalienable rights or freedoms endowed by the Creator. They made it clear that denial of these freedoms marked a government (foreign or domestic) as "an absolute Tyranny."

Rights v. Liberties

In general, civil liberties are freedoms to do certain things without restraint from the government. Ordinarily, however, there is no implication that private individuals or agencies may not impose restraints. A person, for example, may express his opinions freely insofar as governmental action is concerned, but this liberty does not imply a duty imposed on a newspaper to publish those opinions. In this regard civil liberties may be distinguished from civil rights.

States, in the exercise of their police power, may enact laws to prohibit public officials and private individuals from discriminating against persons because of their race, color, religion, sex, age, physical handicaps, or national origin in employment opportunities; in offering of accommodations in hotels, restaurants, common carriers, and other places of public resort; in educational institutions; and in housing. These laws, known as civil rights acts and fair employment or fair housing acts, have been enacted in many U.S. localities and by Congress.

Most parts of the United States Constitution have been interpreted as prohibiting state action (but not the action of individuals as private citizens) that discriminates against persons for reasons of race or color. (The Thirteenth Amendment, which prohibits slavery, however, does include private action.) Racial discrimination by states—for example, in public education—has been held to be a violation of the "equal protection clause" of the Fourteenth Amendment, as in *Brown* v. *Board of Education of Topeka* (1954). Similarly, discrimination by the federal government was held to violate the due process clause of the Fifth Amendment, in *Bolling* v. *Sharpe* (1954). These decisions, though they stem from constitutional guarantees and not from laws passed by legislatures, are usually conceived of as involving civil rights rather than civil liberties.

Civil rights, generally speaking, may be viewed as attempts to give meaning to the idea of equality. Civil liberties, on the other hand, stem from the idea of freedom. Civil rights and civil liberties are intimately related, however, and perhaps are interdependent. A person who is denied equality is not likely to feel free, and a person who is denied freedom is likely to find that he has also lost equality. The distinction between civil rights and civil liberties is therefore more philosophical and academic than practical.

Natural Law Theory

The assertion in American law of limits on government emerged from the belief that every person has rights or freedoms that are so intimately connected with his nature as a human being that to take them away would be to deprive him of part of his humanity. They enter into the very nature of the person.

Any enumeration of specific civil liberties or basic human freedoms depends upon the character of the culture and on time and place. Freedom of speech, for example, could not seem very significant among illiterate peoples. Freedom of the press took on importance only after the widespread use

Black and white students study together in an elementary school in Topeka, Kans., in 1954. The city voted to abolish segregation while its case, Brown v. Board of Education of Topeka, *was before the Supreme Court. In the landmark decision the Court ruled that separate educational facilities were inherently unequal and in violation of the Fourteenth Amendment.*

of the printing press. The root idea, however, of rights or freedoms inherent in a person and not subject to destruction by a prince or ruler was found in many diverse cultures and civilizations. Sometimes this assertion of basic freedoms was expressed briefly as a belief in human dignity, or in the biblical idea that every person was made in the image of God, or in the existence of natural law and natural rights.

All of these beliefs led to the position that there are limits on government or that government is the result of a "social contract" in which only certain powers are delegated to the ruler. Rulership was thought to be vested in a government of laws and not of men; the laws of a ruler were subject to judgment under a higher law.

In the seventeenth and eighteenth centuries the theory of natural law led to the theory of natural rights. As stated by the English philosopher John Locke (1632–1704), the social contract among members of society and between society and government provided that government had, as one of its chief ends, the protection of the lives, liberties, and estates of the members of society. Locke added that by property he meant "that property which men have in their persons as well as goods" (*Second Treatise of Government*, 1689). For the vindication of their "inherent and inalienable" rights (Jefferson's phrasing of Locke's doctrine in the original draft of the Declaration of Independence) the people should look to "parliament"; if this failed, they had the right to resort to revolution.

While the British have looked to Parliament for vindication of their fundamental liberties, some other countries, notably the United States, have looked chiefly to the courts for the protection of their fundamental liberties. This alternative became more possible with the development of written constitutions and bills of rights. Into these documents went the religious, philosophical, and judicial conceptions that had been developed over many centuries, among diverse civilizations, peoples, and religions.

Partial precedents for written bills of rights existed in the Magna Carta (1215), the English Bill of Rights (1689), and the Declaration of Independence (1776). The Virginia Declaration of Rights (adopted one month before the Declaration of Independence) is particularly notable because Virginia was a leading colony and because the language of the document was especially felicitous. It declared that "all men are by nature equally free and independent," and that they have certain inherent rights of which they cannot deprive themselves or their posterity—"namely, the enjoyment of life and liberty, with the means of acquiring and possessing property, and pursuing and obtaining happiness and safety." Specific civil liberties enumerated included the freedom of the press, the free exercise of religion, and the fact that no man was to be deprived of his liberty except by the law of the land or by the judgment of his peers.

The Constitution of the United States, drafted in 1787 and ratified in 1788, contained some safeguards of personal liberty —a guarantee of the privilege of the writ of habeas corpus (to be freed from unlawful imprisonment); a prohibition on bills of attainder (laws punishing named individuals); ex post facto laws (which made actions criminal after their occurrence); and test oaths. But the Constitution did not include a bill of rights. Alexander Hamilton and the other authors of *The Federalist* papers, while approving these guarantees, justified the omission of a bill of rights by arguing that, since the federal government was to have only delegated powers, there was no need to reserve to the people powers not surrendered by them: "For why declare that things shall not be done which there is no power to do?" (*The Federalist* No. 84). The ratifying states, however, were not convinced. They demanded a bill of rights, and in 1791 the Constitution was amended to include the Bill of Rights.

It is worth noting here that at the same time, in 1789, at the beginning of the French Revolution, the National Assembly of France issued a Declaration of the Rights of Man and of the Citizen. This declaration stated that there were certain sacred rights of men and of citizens—among them, that men are born, and always continue, free and equal in respect to their rights; that the end of all political associations is the preservation of the natural and imprescriptible rights of man, including liberty, property, security, and the resistance of oppression; that political or civil liberty consists in the power of doing whatever does not injure another; that the law ought to prohibit only actions hurtful to society; that no man should be accused, arrested, or held in confinement, except in cases determined by law and according to the forms which it has prescribed; that no one ought to be punished except under a law promulgated before the offense; that a man is presumed innocent until he has been convicted; that no man ought to be molested because of his opinions, including his religious opinions, as long as their expression does not disturb the public order established by the law; and that every citizen may speak, write, and publish freely his thoughts and opinions, provided he is responsible for abuse of this liberty, in cases determined by law.

Following the example of the French Declaration and of the U.S. Declaration of Independence and Bill of Rights, many countries in the nineteenth and twentieth centuries adopted written constitutions with bills of rights. Other countries, influenced in various degrees by the example of Great Britain, adopted no written constitutions (for example, Israel) or adopted written constitutions containing no bills of rights (for example, Australia, Canada, and New Zealand). In these countries fundamental rights are nonetheless recognized and guaranteed by common law, court decisions, and legislation that reflect deep traditions. Great Britain's influence is somewhat ironic; respected British judges and political leaders have urged in recent years that a written bill of rights, with provisions for judicial review, is necessary because of the inability of the common-law system to keep up with the technology of oppression. Despite such arguments, no action has been taken.

The Bill of Rights

The Bill of Rights of the U.S. Constitution was demanded not only by the states but also by Thomas Jefferson, who perhaps was influenced by the revolutionary atmosphere of France, where he lived from 1784 to 1789. Jefferson was the author of the Virginia bill for the establishment of religious freedom. In it he expressed the conviction that the opinions of man cannot be coerced. That measure, with the support of James Madison (later the fourth U.S. president, 1809–17), was adopted in 1786. Writing to Madison from Paris in 1787, Jefferson stated that "a bill of rights is what the people are entitled to against every government on earth."

As adopted in 1791, the first ten amendments to the Constitution constitute the Bill of Rights. The two most sweeping and far-reaching guarantees provide: that "Congress shall make no law respecting an establishment of religion, or prohibiting the free exercise thereof; or abridging the freedom of speech, or of the press; or the right of the people peaceably to assemble, and to petition the Government for a redress of grievances" (First Amendment); and that "no person shall be . . . deprived of life, liberty, or property, without due process of law; nor shall private property be taken for public use without just compensation" (Fifth Amendment).

Other guarantees are: that there shall be security against unreasonable searches and seizures affecting persons, houses, papers, and effects; that no warrants shall be issued except upon probable cause, supported by oath or affirmation, and describing the place to be searched and the person or things to be seized; that no person shall be held to answer for a capital or otherwise infamous crime except on presentment or indictment by a grand jury; that no person shall twice be put in jeopardy of life or limb for the same offense, or be compelled to be a witness against himself in any criminal case. In criminal cases, the defendant is guaranteed the right to a speedy and public trial by an impartial jury, to be informed of the nature of the accusation against him, to be confronted with the witnesses against him, to have compulsory process for obtaining witnesses in his favor, and to have the assistance of defense counsel. Excessive bail, excessive fines, and cruel and unusual punishments are prohibited.

Since the United States is a federal republic, the courts were faced with the question of whether the Bill of Rights was a limit on only the federal government or on both the federal government and state governments. In *Barron* v. *Baltimore* (1833) the Supreme Court limited the effectiveness of the Bill of Rights to the federal government. After the Civil War, however, three important amendments were added to the Constitution that undermined the *Barron* decision. The Thirteenth Amendment prohibits slavery and involuntary servitude. The Fourteenth Amendment provides that "No State shall make or enforce any law which shall abridge the privileges or immunities of citizens of the United States; nor shall any State deprive any person of life, liberty, or property, without due process of law; nor deny to any person within its jurisdiction the equal protection of the laws." The Fifteenth Amendment provides that the right of citizens to vote shall not be denied or abridged by the United States or any state on account of race, color, or previous condition of servitude.-The Civil War amendments do not expressly make applicable to the states the guarantees of the Bill of Rights. The Supreme Court, however, held that the terms *liberty* and *due process of law* in the Fourteenth Amendment make available to criminal defendants certain provisions of the first ten amendments against state action. The Court early limited such protection to basic rights that were "implicit in the concept of ordered liberty"—for, if they were sacrificed, "neither liberty nor justice would exist" (*Palko* v. *Connecticut*, 1937). The freedoms of the First Amendment, for example, have been held to be protected by the Fourteenth Amendment against encroachment by the states, in *Gitlow* v. *New York* (1925). The complete meaning of what the Court has called the "spacious language" of the due process clause has been hotly debated among the justices since *Palko* was decided. Some members of the Court, notably Hugo L. Black and William O. Douglas, maintained after World War II that the Fourteenth Amendment incorporates all of the freedoms guaranteed by the Bill of Rights, but this has always been a minority view.

Notwithstanding the division in the Court over the general theory of incorporation, the Court extended, in a series of notable decisions, the reach of constitutional guarantees so broadly that the states became limited almost as much as the federal government. Thus, the Fifth Amendment guarantee against compulsory self-incrimination now limits the states, as in *Malloy* v. *Hogan* (1964), through a rule that makes involuntary confessions inadmissible as evidence at trial, as in *Miranda* v. *Arizona* (1966). So, too, the Fourth Amendment guarantee against unreasonable searches and seizures, as exemplified in *Mapp* v. *Ohio* (1961), the Sixth Amendment guarantees of trial by jury, in *Duncan* v. *Louisiana* (1968), and with assistance of counsel, in *Gideon* v. *Wainwright* (1963), and the Eighth Amendment guarantee against cruel and unusual punishment, in *Robinson* v. *California* (1962), also apply to the states. These decisions, giving further security to the person, affected the administration of criminal justice enormously and were a highly significant part of the record of the Supreme Court under Chief Justice Earl Warren (1953–69).

Civil Rights

American civil rights have expanded legal benefits in several ways. First, the classes of persons who are the beneficiaries of civil rights have grown. The earliest groups protected were blacks and aliens. Next came persons distinguished by their religion or creed (Roman Catholics, Mormons, Jews) and persons identified by their ethnic background, for example, persons of Italian origin and people with Spanish surnames. More recently, women, or persons discriminated against by reason of their sex, have benefited. One of the latest groups to benefit has been those discriminated against by reason of their age: Congress in 1967 enacted the Age Discrimination in Employment Act, which prohibits job discrimination against persons who are forty years of age and older.

Second, there has been a great expansion in the interests protected. The first civil rights laws protected against discrimination in places of public accommodation or entertainment. The pattern for this type of law goes back to a statute of Massachusetts adopted on May 16, 1865. Eighteen states had such laws by 1900, and twenty-four had them by 1960. The next interest to be protected was employment. Executive order 8802, issued by President Franklin D. Roosevelt on June 25, 1941, established the first Fair Employment Practices Committee (FEPC) and the principle that individuals were to be employed "without discrimination because of race, creed, color, or national origin." This was the forerunner of state fair employment practices laws. The first such law was that of New York in 1945. It prohibited discrimination by employers, unions, and employment agencies. Opportunity for employment without discrimination was declared a civil right. By 1970 there were similar laws in thirty-nine states.

The next interest to be protected was education. Again New York was a pioneer: in 1948 it enacted the first fair educational practices law. New Jersey and Massachusetts followed in 1949, as did some other states in the North and West in subsequent years. Another major interest touched by civil rights principles was housing. New York in 1955 again became the first state to ban discrimination in certain types of housing in which state or federal financing was involved. The first prohibition of discrimination in private housing came in 1959 with laws enacted in Colorado, Connecticut, Massachusetts, and Oregon. New York City in 1957 and Pittsburgh in 1958 adopted local ordinances against such discrimination. Since the 1940s, therefore, it has been demonstrated that the principle of civil rights is open-ended—both as to persons affected and as to interests protected.

With respect to the development of national law, as distinguished from action taken by individual states, three obstacles, two constitutional and one political, stood in the way. First was the principle of "separate but equal" facilities upheld by the Supreme Court in *Plessy* v. *Ferguson* (1896). That case upheld the constitutionality of a statute providing for separate but equal accommodations on railroads for white and black passengers. It was a decision that validated racial segregation enforced by law.

Second was the principle that the Fourteenth Amendment requirement of due process of law and of equal protection of the law was a guarantee only against improper state action—that the provisions of the amendment were in no way directed at private action. This principle was formulated in the *Civil Rights Cases* of 1883; in it the Supreme Court held unconstitutional the Civil Rights Act of 1875 (which provided that all persons shall be entitled to full and equal enjoyment of accommodations and privileges in inns, public conveyances, and theaters and other places of public amusement). The court held that, while Congress had the power to enforce the Fourteenth Amendment through appropriate laws, the laws had to be directed against discriminatory state action, not private action. Finally, there was the overwhelming political obstacle that blocked federal civil rights legislation for more than a century, namely, the power of Southern legislators in Congress, through the seniority system and the threat of the filibuster, to obstruct effectively the passage of civil rights acts.

The first radical change in this formidable structure came with the Supreme Court's unanimous decision in the historic case of *Brown* v. *Board of Education of Topeka* (1954). In that case, the Court pushed aside the "separate but equal" principle and held that racial segregation in the public schools, when imposed by law, was unconstitutional. The reason the Court gave for disregarding *Plessy* v. *Ferguson* was simple: "separate but equal," the Court said, is "inherently unequal." In reaching this conclusion, the Court relied on social science data and the evidence of prominent sociologists and psychologists. Such reasoning was controversial among both politicians and legal scholars.

Whatever the merits of the reasoning, however, the mandate of the Court was clear and the effect of the decision was earthshaking: racial segregation was outlawed in the schools of seventeen Southern and border states (and the District of Columbia), where 8 million white and 2.5 million black pupils attended segregated elementary and secondary schools. Subsequent cases applied the *Brown* principle to outlaw racial segregation in state colleges and universities, interstate and local transportation, municipal golf courses, recreational facilities and municipal parks, public beaches and bathhouses, restaurants in public buildings, and other facilities. Miscegenation laws were declared unconstitutional. The vitality of the *Brown* case depended on the federal courts that applied it, and credit for its vigorous, even courageous, enforcement lies not so much with the Supreme Court as with the federal trial and appellate judges in the areas most deeply affected by racial segregation.

The second great change came from Congress with the enactment of the Civil Rights Act of 1964. Congress had passed civil rights acts in 1957 and 1960, but they were extremely limited in scope. The 1964 statute is certainly one of the most important and far-ranging in U.S. history and in the history of social legislation in general. The act prohibits discrimination or segregation in places of public accommodation on account of race, color, religion, or national origin. It applies to hotels and motels for transients, restaurants and other eating places, movie and other theaters, concert halls, sports arenas and stadiums, and other places of exhibition or entertainment. The establishments reached by the act are those that in some way are touched by interstate commerce, including travel, trade, commerce, transportation, and communication.

Like the Civil Rights Act of 1875, which was struck down by the Supreme Court in 1883, the 1964 statute reaches businesses that are privately owned and operated and that involve

Martin Luther King attends the signing ceremony of the Civil Rights Act of 1964. The statute is one of the most far-reaching in U.S. history, forbidding discrimination in public accommodations.

no state action. The constitutional foundation for the 1964 act, however, was the commerce power of Congress and not the Fourteenth Amendment. On this basis the constitutionality of the act was upheld in the *Heart of Atlanta* (1964) case. The Supreme Court expressly recognized that Congress had concerned itself with discrimination in the act, but it went on to hold that this fact did not detract from the power of Congress to regulate commerce, and so the 1883 decision was held to be irrelevant to the central constitutional question in the case.

In addition to prohibiting racial segregation or discrimination in privately owned places of public accommodation or entertainment, the act also deals with desegregation of public facilities, desegregation of public education, and voting rights. Title VII, which covers equal employment opportunity, deserves special attention because of its great importance. It forbids employment-related discrimination on the basis of race, color, religion, sex, or national origin by any employer whose business involves interstate commerce. The prohibition extends also to labor unions and employment agencies. The Supreme Court has construed the act to prohibit not only direct discrimination but also indirect (for example, verbal reasoning tests for electrical company linemen in *Griggs* v. *Duke Power Co.*, 1971).

The 1964 act originated in a milder version sponsored by President John F. Kennedy, but the real pressure for its passage came from President Lyndon B. Johnson following the sit-ins, freedom marches, and other demonstrations of the mid-1960s led by Dr. Martin Luther King, Jr. Sit-ins began at Greensboro, N.C., in 1960 and soon developed into a national movement. On Aug. 28, 1963, Washington, D.C., had one of the largest demonstrations in its history when two hundred thousand persons, mostly blacks, gathered from all parts of the country to demand full civil rights for blacks.

Momentum for civil rights continued with the enactment, in 1965, of a strong Voting Rights Act and with the passage of the Civil Rights Act of 1968. The latter act included prohibitions on discrimination in the sale or rental of housing and in the making of commercial real estate loans or in the financing of housing. The act also prohibits discriminatory advertising of housing for sale or rental. The constitutionality of Title VIII, which is, in effect, a fair housing practices law, was sustained by implication in *Jones* v. *Mayer Co.* (1968). In

The civil rights movement of the 1960s reached its climax when two hundred thousand persons marched on Washington, D.C., to protest racial discrimination.

Jones the Supreme Court upheld a civil rights act of 1866 that barred all racial discrimination, private as well as public, in the sale or rental of property. The statute was upheld under the Thirteenth Amendment on the basis that the essence of civil freedom included the right to purchase, sell, lease, and convey property. The theory was that, when the amendment ended slavery and involuntary servitude, it also ended any impediment to blacks enjoying these basic civil rights. The principle of *Jones* v. *Mayer* was extended by the Court in 1976 to bar discriminatory admission practices of purely private schools on the theory that the right to contract for educational services was essentially the same as the right to buy property (*McCrary* v. *Runyon*).

In *University of California Regents* v. *Bakke* (1978), the Court held that a white medical school applicant, Allan Bakke, was discriminated against by an admissions program that voluntarily set aside a certain number of places in each freshman class for minorities. "Preferring members of any one group for no reason other than race or ethnic origin is discriminating for its own sake," the Court ruled. While the

Bakke decision appeared to be a blanket rejection of the use of racial or ethnic quotas in affirmative action plans, it left open to question the legality of such programs that were outside the area of college admissions and not based on quotas. And, though stating that race was a legitimate criterion for admissions, the Court warned that it could not be the *sole* criterion without running afoul of the constitution and civil rights laws.

9.
The Legal Status of Women

Complete equality of the sexes has been advocated since the Greek philosopher Plato wrote his *Republic* in the fourth century before Christ. The civilizations of China, India, and Rome, and later the various renaissances of western Europe, could boast small groups of highly cultivated women, but only since the mid-nineteenth century has there been any substantial progress toward equality for women. The spheres in which women have been forced to fight for equality include education, suffrage, property rights, industry, the professions, and public life.

The status of women is as dependent on prejudice as it is on law. In western Europe and in North America, where the idea of the equality of the sexes first took practical root, a change in status preceded legislation and—with the important exception of suffrage—was often not dependent on law. Once changes had been made, however, an interlocking network of laws guaranteed the new position. Although it was education that pried open the door of political emancipation for women in Europe—particularly in the United Kingdom—it was social economics in the United States. At the end of the nineteenth century the enormous increase in population brought about fundamental changes in the industrial and social structure of the country and a migration to the towns.

The United States was the first country to admit women into any of the professions, and in all of the states there has been legislation permitting women to engage in civil professions and occupations. Teaching was the first profession to include women; after the experiment succeeded in private institutions, state schools began hiring women teachers in 1839. This action was connected with a gradual movement to establish secondary education for girls, which became free and universal by about 1870. In the 1890s it was estimated that ten percent of all women teachers were high school graduates. Indiana was the first state, in 1907, to require that teachers be high school graduates in order to qualify for a license.

The first U.S. woman to be licensed as a doctor was Elizabeth Blackwell at Geneva, N.Y., in 1849. In 1850 Female (now Woman's) Medical College of Pennsylvania in Philadelphia was incorporated. By 1890 there were three schools offering medical training for women only, and three older institutions had become coeducational. Between 1820 and 1890 all of the states admitted women to the bar. Beginning in 1848 married women gained the right to own property and to make contracts as though they were single. In 1874 legislation was passed in Massachusetts, the most important manufacturing state, limiting the number of hours worked by women. In the 1880s and 1890s other states followed, although only three states made the law enforceable. Equal pay laws were introduced in about twenty states. A striking feature of the Civil Rights Act of 1964 was the "Equal Employment Opportunity" section (Title VII), which prohibited discrimination on the basis of sex. In March 1972 Congress passed the Equal Rights Amendment—prohibiting discrimination based on sex—and sent it to the states for ratification.

Women's suffrage was finally achieved in 1920 with the Nineteenth Amendment to the Constitution. The first woman to hold a Cabinet seat was Frances Perkins of New York, who was named secretary of labor in 1933. Clare Boothe Luce was named U.S. ambassador to Italy in 1953, and in 1962 Katie Louchheim was appointed deputy assistant secretary of state for public affairs. The record has improved dramatically in the legislative and executive branches of government since

Secretary of Labor Frances Perkins, the first woman to hold a Cabinet seat, meets with workers at a steel mill in Pittsburgh to get information first-hand.

the mid-1960s, although the federal judiciary in the late 1970s still had only a few women district judges and one appeals court judge—Shirley M. Hufstedler of Los Angeles. The first black woman elected to the House of Representatives was Shirley Chisholm (D., N.Y.) in 1968. One-third of all foreign service personnel are women. The last substantial limitation on the right of women to hold public office was removed in 1942 when Oklahoma ceased to bar women from office as governor, lieutenant governor, or attorney general.

Accomplishments of the Women's Movement

One of the most important legal symbols of equal rights for women is the Nineteenth Amendment, which provides: "The right of citizens of the United States to vote shall not be denied or abridged by the United States or by any State on account of sex." The history of the amendment reflects the difficulty encountered by the early women's movement. Agitation for women's suffrage began in the mid-nineteenth century and was successful in ten states, but the progress was slow. The equal suffrage amendment had been sought for more than a decade before it was finally ratified in 1920.

When the Women's Rights Convention met in 1848 at Seneca Falls, N.Y., the delegates protested against disenfranchisement, the legal incapacity of women after marriage, the double standard in morals, employment disabilities, the denial of equal educational opportunities, and the subordination of women in church governance. The first of these grievances ended with the Nineteenth Amendment. The other grievances persisted in varying degrees into the 1960s and 1970s and became matters of public concern and discussion, as activists engaged in demonstrations with sit-ins, petitions, and strikes. Among their demands were equal pay for equal work, legalization of elective abortion, passage of an equal rights amendment to the Constitution, twenty-four-hour child-care centers, and the admission of women to colleges and universities that were closed to them. The ground for this movement had been prepared in part by social and technological developments, such as the creation of a large class of educated women, the involvement of women in the work force (approximately 40 million out of 100 million workers in the United States were women in 1976), the availability of reliable and convenient contraceptives, the virtual disappearance of the need of physical strength for economic usefulness and advancement, and the reduced role of women as homemakers and housekeepers, which freed them for other activities.

A measure of the movement's success is demonstrated by the fact that before 1964 only two states prohibited discrimination in employment because of sex but that in 1970 there were such laws in twenty-five states and equal pay laws in forty. In part, a push toward this development came from the passage by Congress of the Equal Pay Act of 1963 (as an amendment to the Fair Labor Standards Act of 1938). While the number of exceptions and qualifications in the federal act leaves the door open for evasions, the act does establish an important principle, which has been influential. Even more significant, of course, was the Civil Rights Act of 1964.

It must be noted that the federal rights act and most state civil rights acts do not prohibit sexual discrimination in places of public entertainment or accommodation, but when such discrimination has been challenged in the courts, the discrimination has been declared illegal. A notable decision on this point was that of a federal court in 1970, which held that women had a constitutional right to equal treatment at McSorley's Bar in New York City—famous until then as an alehouse for men only. Soon after this decision a New York City ordinance was adopted to prohibit sexual discrimination in places of public entertainment.

In an important decision made in 1971, the U.S. Supreme Court applied the equal protection clause of the Fourteenth Amendment to a state statute that gave men preference over women in the appointment of an administrator of an estate. The Court fell short of banning such laws outright: in effect it held that it would consider them on a case-by-case basis to determine if they were reasonable. This approach to the constitutional problem through the equal protection clause represents a position taken by some opponents of the proposed Equal Rights Amendment, which provides that equality of rights under the law shall not be denied or abridged by the country or by any state on account of sex.

The proposed amendment has had a checkered and controversial history. It was first brought before Congress in 1923. In 1950 and 1953 it passed the Senate with the Hayden rider, which provided that the amendment not be construed to impair any rights, benefits, or exemptions conferred by law on women. In 1971 a Senate judiciary subcommittee amended the bill to allow distinctions "based on physiological or functional differences" between the sexes. The main intention of the proposals to change the text of the amendment was to save labor laws that had been previously enacted to protect women workers from long hours, night work, heavy lifting, and other presumed hazards. Many liberal women's leaders, such as Eleanor Roosevelt, opposed such an amendment out of a concern for the preservation of these protective labor laws. More recently, proponents of the amendment and women's liberation leaders have argued that the special laws, by keeping women out of jobs, have been hurtful and not protective; that they perpetuate a paternalistic attitude that stands in the way of equality; and that what is good in protective labor laws for women should be extended to men.

Some constitutional authorities have argued that the Equal Rights Amendment is unnecessary and that reliance should instead be placed on the equal protection clause of the Fourteenth Amendment as reinterpreted by the Supreme Court in the light of present knowledge, present values, and revised legislation enacted by the states and Congress. This argument has withered somewhat in the last few years, however, as the Court has consistently refused to apply the equal protection clause to women with the same vigor that it has applied the clause to protect racial groups. The Court has held, for example, that industry "income protection plans" that pay for major and minor surgery under sick leave provisions but not for pregnancy and related disabilities do not discriminate

Demonstrators march in support of the Equal Rights Amendment at a women's rally held in Chicago, Illinois, in 1978.

unconstitutionally against women. In 1976 the Court upheld such plans as being consistent with the Civil Rights Act of 1964 (Title VII). The Equal Rights Amendment must be ratified by thirty-eight states in order to become law. It was still a few short of that in the late 1970s, but the date for ratification was extended from March 1979 to June 1982.

Recent Developments

While the constitutional argument has continued, feminists have attacked sexual inequality in hundreds of cases brought against colleges and universities, employers, and owners of places of entertainment or public accommodation and have done so with a substantial degree of success. Symbolic of the new order are these developments: in the late 1960s and early 1970s many all-male colleges and universities, including Yale and Princeton, opened their doors to women students; in many such institutions the curriculum now includes a program of women's studies; many institutions of higher learning and professional schools search actively for women to appoint to their faculties. Other professions have demonstrated the same concern. Large corporate law firms, for example, have sought young women lawyers—not infrequently under pressure from the Equal Employment Opportunity Commission (EEOC) or the courts—to break down formerly all-male bastions. Progress in the legal profession has been rapid in recent years, although the Harvard Law School graduated its first woman as recently as the 1950s. Up until the late 1960s there had been only one woman law clerk to the Supreme Court of the United States.

Probably the most controversial issue in women's rights is abortion. In 1973 the Supreme Court struck down as unconstitutional laws in Texas and Georgia that criminalized elective abortions. The Court held, in effect, that the decision to abort within the first twelve weeks of pregnancy is a private one, to be made by a woman and her physician, exempt from state interference. In 1976 the Court extended the ruling to make the decision exempt from requirements of parental or spousal consent. In a landmark decision in 1977, however, the Court held that the states are not required by the Constitution to pay for elective abortions from public funds. The effect of the decision, practically speaking, is to make "abortion on demand" available only to those who can afford it. It was estimated that approximately twenty-five percent of the reported abortions in 1976 had been paid for with public funds.

III. Law in Business

"The fundamental principles which govern the handling of postage stamps and millions of dollars are exactly the same. They are the common law of business, and the whole practice of commerce is founded on them. They are so simple that a fool can't learn them; so hard that a lazy man won't."

—Philip D. Armour

10.
Corporations and Corporate Law

A corporation is a group of persons authorized by law to act as a unit. It may be a public body, as is commonly the case in Great Britain, or a business enterprise, as is usually the case in the United States. It may also be an educational institution, such as a college or university, a labor union, or a charitable foundation. A public corporation is an agency of government established to carry on certain functions of a business nature, such as the Reconstruction Finance Corporation in the United States.

A corporation is a fictitious legal person. As such, it has a corporate name, followed by the word *incorporated* or the abbreviation *Inc*. In this name the corporation may sue and be sued and may hold and transfer property. In the eyes of the law, therefore, the group has an existence independent of its individual members; this is the distinguishing feature of the legal concept of a "corporation." Its continuity of existence gives the corporation as a form of business enterprise a clear advantage over a partnership, which comes to an end with the death of a partner.

Business corporations divide their capital stock into shares. Shares are often purchased by a large number of investors, each subscribing a relatively small sum. The fact that a corporation's capital is divisible makes it easier for those heading the group to accumulate the large sums of money required by modern industry. Another factor that makes it simpler for corporations to acquire capital is the limited liability of shareholders for the debts of the corporation. In the event of bankruptcy shareholders may lose their investments in the corporation, but all their other property is safe.

Such advantages go far to explain the predominance of the corporate form in modern American economic life, particularly in manufacturing. But they have little relevance to the period of its origins either in Europe or in the United States. To understand how the business corporation developed in the United States, a brief historical sketch, with reference to the European background, is necessary.

Beginnings

Corporations existed long before they were used for business purposes. The more complex societies of the ancient world developed towns, guilds, and colonies; churches and universities appeared in medieval Europe. The idea that one must have the legal authority of the state in order to form a corporate body is also very old. In England the authority of the Crown was essential from the first in forming a business corporation. After the revolution of 1688, the authority of Parliament was needed in any case involving a grant of monopoly or other special privilege. Governments granted charters of incorporation to various private companies mainly to encourage private capital to promote ends that were regarded as public or semipublic in nature—such as voyages of discovery, trade, and colonization.

Corporations existed long before they were used for business purposes—taking the form of towns, guilds, and colonies. In medieval Europe corporations were created for ecclesiastical and educational purposes.

In the American colonies the first corporations took the form of towns, boroughs, and cities. Before the end of the colonial period, a large number of corporations had also been created for ecclesiastical, educational, and charitable purposes. But business corporations were few in number and relatively unimportant. The main reason for this was that the spheres of activity in which business corporations were required were subject to the disposition of the Crown and the Parliament, rather than to local colonial governments. The prevailing doctrine toward merchants and trading was not calculated to inspire the American colonists to become self-sufficient.

Change appeared soon after the colonies won their independence. Between the end of the American Revolution and 1801, state governments created more than three hundred business corporations. Approximately two-thirds of them were established for transportation purposes—to provide inland navigation, turnpikes, and toll bridges. Insurance companies were also created to underwrite the new American trade.

Highway and other public service associations predominated among the early American corporations. This clearly shows the greater sense of responsibility assumed by American political communities after the Revolution. These business corporations, formed for such varied purposes as to supply water, provide fire insurance, and erect flour mills, were no more exclusively profit-seeking associations than were the chartered joint-stock companies with which the English had pioneered in the settlement of America. They were, in fact, quasi-public agencies of the state. Thus, on the whole, the character of most early American corporations reflected the ancient view that charters should be issued only to associations formed to serve the public interest.

During most of the first third of the nineteenth century public service continued to be the chief reason for which business corporations were chartered. The chartering of this kind of corporation was one answer to such obstacles to development as scarce capital and the undeveloped nature of the country. Public interest in "internal improvements" was keen, and state governments responded by granting tax exemptions and other privileges to corporations that were engaged in improving transportation facilities.

As capital accumulated, the line between public interest and private advantage became more sharply visible to the critics of corporate privilege. Abuse crept easily into the prevailing system of obtaining charters. Populist leaders such as President Andrew Jackson fought to put an end to the special privileges enjoyed by corporations. They held that the profit-making opportunities in the growing economy should be open to all on equal terms.

These attacks upon enterprise restrictions had two important consequences. The first was the passage by a number of states of general incorporation laws before the Civil War; free banking laws were also passed. The second was a new tendency to seek charters of incorporation in such expanding fields of enterprise as the manufacturing of carpets, watches, and sewing machines. Along with this development there was a shift of emphasis among business corporations from public service to private profit.

Emergence of the Business Corporation

A rapid increase in charters granted in the 1850s heralded the dawn of the age of the business corporation. Yet it was only the dawn. Industrial techniques that required large capital investment were just being organized in important fields, and they spread slowly among affected firms. Not until after 1835 did expensive metallic textile machinery come into general use. Not until 1839 were the first successful coke-burning smelters built in the United States. As late as 1869 nearly half the mechanical power used in manufacturing came from waterwheels and turbines rather than from steam engines. But it is the spread of new techniques rather than their first appearance that matters in economic growth. Imitation is more important than innovation. And several explanations exist for the imitative lag that occurred, among them the inertia of traditional and less costly methods, ignorance of new techniques, scarcity of technical journals and trained engineers, and unsophisticated cost-accounting techniques. These obstacles were gradually overcome in the post-Civil War years, and mechanized production methods became more widely known. But in the 1860s it was the individual proprietorships and partnerships rather than the corporations that were able to amass the capital required to control most of the resources devoted to manufacturing.

In the second half of the nineteenth century three principal developments gave life to the business corporation. First, there was a phenomenal expansion in manufacturing corporations. This was especially true in such fields as iron and steel, nonferrous metals, textiles, chemicals, and liquor. Indeed, manufacturing corporations constituted a large percentage of all charters granted after 1875. Second, there was a notable growth in the size of the individual unit of enterprise. Finally, during the 1880s there were remarkable changes in administrative organization that marked the emergence of the modern corporation.

In the latter part of the nineteenth century, the growing importance of powerful businessmen paralleled the growth of corporations. A handful of wealthy individuals dominated the industrial scene during this era.

These three major developments pointed to great growth in the economic role of the corporation. But partnerships and sole proprietorships also continued to play substantial roles in economic life. Paralleling the growth of corporations was the towering growth in importance of individual businessmen. It was these men, rather than the corporations, who left their stamp on these years. In the forefront of industrial expansion stood such people as Andrew Carnegie (iron and steel), Gustavus Swift (meat-packing), John D. Rockefeller (oil), James J. Hill (railroads), and J. P. Morgan (investment banking). The business organizations of these individuals often took the form of partnerships during the early years, but for the most part their later careers and those of their successors involved corporations.

Growth of Urban Markets. Corporations increased in number as urban growth opened up markets for manufactured consumer goods. Railroads forged the transcontinental links of this market. The spreading railroad net made it possible for farmers to settle in the West—the last frontier. During the half-century following the Civil War, farmers occupied more land than they had in all the previous years of American history. The use of machinery and scientific techniques in-

In 1869 the Central Pacific and Union Pacific railroads drove the final spike linking the country together with the first transcontinental line. The growing railroad network connected the expanding urban markets and stimulated settlement in the West.

creased the agricultural output of new and fertile lands and quickened the growth of such older cities as New York, Philadelphia, Cincinnati, Cleveland, and St. Louis. It also helped create such new cities as Chicago, Indianapolis, Atlanta, Kansas City, Dallas, Minneapolis, and St. Paul. Between 1840 and 1880 the urban proportion of the total population rose from 11% to 28%; by 1900 it was 40%.

This rapid urban growth intensified demand for the products of industries manufacturing consumer goods. Between 1880 and 1907 many businesses were incorporated for the manufacture of food and kindred products, textile mill products, and other consumer goods. Such industries were the first to be dominated by great business enterprises. By the beginning of the twentieth century, however, a growing number of companies were manufacturing machinery for the use of producers rather than goods for consumers or farmers.

The Corporation and the Fourteenth Amendment. Noneconomic forces also paved the way for corporate expansion and even augmented its scale. After the Jacksonian attack on privileged corporations, several states had (in the 1840s) adopted constitutional provisions requiring incorporation under general laws. By 1875 these provisions were so common that special charters became a thing of the past. Since the new system opened incorporation on equal terms to all, it was considered more democratic than the old. Incorporation was no longer looked upon as a privilege but as a right. A symptom of the change in the climate of values—and a great spur to incorporation—was the U.S. Supreme Court's decision that the word *person* in the Fourteenth Amendment to the Constitution applied to corporations in some instances. Since the Fourteenth Amendment specified that no "person" might be deprived of life, liberty, or property without "due process of law," this and subsequent decisions protected corporations from discriminatory taxation by the states.

Incorporation was used in many cases in which its justification in terms of large capital needs was difficult. Since about 1875 it has been generally true that small incorporations (valued at less than $100,000) have constituted a large percentage of total charters granted; medium-sized incorporations (less than $1 million), a much smaller percentage; and large incorporations, the smallest percentage of all. The great number of incorporations among firms of relatively small authorized capital stock can be explained on the grounds that many large companies were first incorporated as small ones. But whether or not originally incorporated as a large firm, the great modern corporation dominates the field of American industry, and some attention must be paid to the reasons for its rise.

Advances in Technology. The spread of a changing technology was chiefly responsible for the rise of big business. The use of heavy machinery and larger plants required firms of larger size. Despite the fact that the number of manufacturing establishments remained almost unchanged during the 1870s, the amount of capital invested in them rose by two-thirds and the value of industrial output by more than one-half. Since these increased capital costs could most conveniently be raised by dividing the total sums into small shares offered for sale to numerous investors, technological change also abetted the rise of the corporation.

Technological change, however, is not self-generating. In any society that possesses the necessary knowledge and skills and has no legal or organizational obstacles to innovation, such an advance depends primarily upon two conditions. The first, scarcity of labor, has been a relatively constant factor in American economic growth until modern times. The second is an increased demand for goods. Substantial gains in the real earnings of workers and in incomes per person indicate that both factors were operating during the second half of the nineteenth century. Both increased mechanization and an enlarged scale of production were responses to these conditions. The mass demand of a national urban market called forth mass production, together with the means necessary to its achievement.

Competitive Position. Turning out large quantities of standardized goods, larger firms achieved efficiencies that lowered the unit cost of production. In competition with small firms, large companies had many advantages. They could hire more highly skilled managers, market goods more effectively, and finance their own needs more cheaply by using profits retained in the business. At the same time, however, the large firms also had higher overhead costs on fixed capital investment in plants and machinery. Depreciation, interest, and obsolescence eroded capital, which created a difficult situation for railroads as well as for large-scale manufacturers. In times of falling prices, business managers tended to maintain production and compete vigorously for sales at any price rather than allow their heavily burdened plants to remain idle. Sales at low prices provided some income, which was better than none at all. But during a long period of falling prices not only smaller firms but also larger firms of lesser efficiency could have little hope for survival.

The years from 1873 to 1896 were precisely such a period of long-term falling prices. American business became a jungle in which many failed to survive bitterly competitive price wars and ruthlessly sharp business practices. With prices (and railroad rates) being forced down close to cost, it became evident that two paths to survival existed: keeping prices up and keeping costs down. Both required that businesses enter into combinations. To keep prices up, businessmen entered into "horizontal" combinations (usually called syndicates or trusts), with competitors who were in the same stage of production or distribution. "Vertical" combinations, on the other hand, integrated all stages of production and did not involve direct restrictions on competition. The firm that practiced vertical combination by bringing under its control the successive stages of production, from raw materials to end products, was able to compete more vigorously, because this practice lowered marketing and other costs and assured supplies.

Business Combinations. The first attempts at combinations among competitors usually took the form of "gentlemen's agreements." These were normally verbal or informal agreements to set and maintain prices, although sometimes they included common policies on cash discounts and other trade practices. When businessmen could not agree informally on the object of the combination, they favored written contractual agreements known as "pools." Pools were formed for various purposes. Sometimes, as in a patent pool, the use of a new device or process was confined to a restricted group. In a profits pool, profits were paid into a central fund and divided up on the basis of percentage of total sales in a given period. Probably the main use of a pool was as a device to restrict output. This was done by dividing the total market and assigning to each producer a portion of it. Sometimes division was made on the basis of output, and sometimes it was territorial. While pools had not been unknown before the Civil War, they were little used until after 1875. In the 1880s and 1890s they were to be found in the important industries that made salt, meat products, whiskey, explosives, steel rails, structural steel, cast-iron pipe, and tobacco products. The only serious difficulty with the use of pools was that they were regarded as illegal under the English common law that was recognized in every U.S. state except Louisiana.

Both gentlemen's agreements and pools may be said to have "worked," if only temporarily. But these comparatively loose forms of collusion had serious disadvantages: to the degree that they were successful in raising prices and achieving high, "monopoly" profits, they encouraged new firms to enter the field. Furthermore, one of the main aims of collusion was to maintain price levels during periods of deflation, but it was precisely at such times that the temptation to violate agreements was strongest. Some better system was required, and business managers found it in more closely knit arrangements.

Trusts and Antitrust Legislation

The first and most famous of the new agreements—the business trust—was worked out in the depression-ridden 1870s for John D. Rockefeller and his Standard Oil Company. Employing ruthlessly competitive business practices, Rockefeller and his associates had succeeded during the 1870s in gaining control of more than ninety percent of the oil-refining capacity of the country. In 1882, three years after they had formed the Standard Oil trust under the laws of Ohio, Rockefeller and his associates induced the shareholders of forty oil companies to turn their shares over to nine trustees. The trustees thereby acquired voting control of all forty companies. In place of stock, the former owners received "trust certificates" entitling them to dividends. This device proved so profitable and so effective as a means of centralizing control over an industry that it was soon widely imitated. During the 1880s trusts were formed in the tobacco, sugar, whiskey, cotton oil, linseed oil, and lead industries.

The fatal defect of trusts was that the agreements were a matter of public record. Since, in the eyes of the common law, conspiracies in restraint of trade or attempts to gain a monopoly were illegal, the prospects of longevity for trusts were not good. A number of lawsuits were begun in the 1880s; in one of them, the supreme court of Ohio ordered the Standard Oil Company to withdraw from the trust on the ground that it was attempting to create a monopoly. It became clear that some other form of combination would have to be used in place of the trust. The solution to this problem was a form of business organization that some states had previously created by special act—the holding company.

Holding Companies. New Jersey revised its general incorporation laws (1888–89) to allow corporations to purchase and hold the securities of one or more subsidiary corporations. It proved to be fairly easy for the resulting "holding companies" to bring a number of previously independent firms under unified control. Voting stock often was so widely distributed that it was possible to exercise effective control by purchasing less than fifty percent of it. New Jersey's Holding Company Act proved so successful in bolstering that state's finances with revenues from incorporation fees that other states soon "liberalized" their corporation laws in an effort to attract business. Few state laws at the time required corporations to divulge significant information to the investing public. It was only after many unprotected investors had been swindled, stock values had been misrepresented, and other abuses by large corporations had taken place that the states, around the turn of the century, abandoned their permissive attitudes and began requiring increased disclosure.

The widespread legalization of the holding company did more than provide a device that enabled competitors to form horizontal combinations: it also gave firms a means of integrating vertically. The nature of the need for some such type of legal device can more clearly be seen by considering the specific case of the consumer goods industries.

Before the rise of a national market individual consumer goods firms relied on commission agents to obtain materials as well as to sell the finished products whenever markets were located more than a few miles from the factory. Their first reaction to the emergence of a national market was to enter into agreements with firms that performed one specific function—such as marketing or distribution. Like the early forms of horizontal combination (gentlemen's agreements and pools), these agreements proved hard to enforce, and resources were not utilized effectively. What was needed was a tighter control of the stream of resources than a mere federation of firms could provide. Also needed was a legal form of business organization that would permit individual firms to conduct their operations on a national scale. Men like Gustavus Swift in meat-packing and others with relatively new products moved toward vertical integration by creating nationwide sales and distribution systems and then building their own purchasing organizations. This kind of vertical integration followed the adoption of the holding company, which provided the necessary legal form.

No matter what the sequence, however, the arrangement of all operations under the control of a single, centralized management raised, in turn, the problem of how to make that control as efficient as possible. This was a problem in business administration, and the successful solution of it produced the modern corporation. The problem had two parts: the need to manage operations that were geographically far apart and the need to coordinate all operations within the firm. To fulfill these needs required a clear distinction between the functions of both field and headquarters offices and also a careful assignment of responsibilities at both levels.

Form of Corporate Organization. The headquarters of business enterprises had been slow in developing. In the early nineteenth century the typical business figure had been the merchant in foreign trade. Needing no large force of permanent employees, he relied mainly on the services of commission agents. Early nineteenth-century industrial enterprises used commission agents to buy their raw materials and sell their finished goods although sometimes they used the selling services of wholesalers. The industrial headquarters, too, were small. As markets expanded from local to regional dimensions, some pre-Civil War firms began to divide their headquarters into various departments. The vertical integration movement accelerated this process of departmentalization. It also obliged businessmen to work out problems of coordination between headquarters and field; they managed this by providing a separate administrative department for each major activity: production or purchasing of raw materials, manufacturing, marketing, and finance.

At the head of each department there was a specialist, often a vice-president, in the activity for which the department was responsible. Each department head had two duties: he had to be responsible for the broader development of his department, and he had to cooperate as a member of an executive committee composed of all department heads, the president, and the chairman of the board of directors. The executive committee, in turn, had three functions. It coordinated the various activities of the enterprise—between departments and between headquarters and field. It made plans for the maintenance and expansion of the enterprise as a whole. And it appraised the performance of the entire organization.

In doing these things, the executive committee came to rely more and more on accounting and statistical information about output, purchases, costs, and sales. The extensive operations of the modern corporation thus permitted a certain amount of specialization in the performance of various managerial functions. Specialization usually meant greater proficiency in each of them. For example, expert accounting techniques introduced scientific procedures, increasing efficiency. Thus, combining specialization in function with centralization of the administrative offices, the modern corporation offered great competitive advantages to firms that adopted its procedures. Other leading firms in the same industry were practically forced to adopt similar organizational structures. Smaller companies, unable to compete except in small and specialized markets, were absorbed or forced into bankruptcy.

Sherman Antitrust Act. These developments did not escape the notice of the general public. Court actions against trusts, together with newspaper attacks on them, whipped public opinion to a high pitch of resentment. The very word *trust* became a synonym for *monopoly*, and by the mid-1890s some seventeen states had passed antitrust laws. Antitrust sentiment was probably strongest in the Middle West, with its numerous farmers. But it was found throughout the country, especially among small businessmen who had been bankrupted by the harsh methods of the trust builders. Huge increases in agricultural production, without accompanying increases in demand, had brought low prices to farmers ever since 1869. The prices that farmers had to pay for goods and services, however, did not undergo a comparable decline. High prices for industrial goods, as well as other things, and the evidence of collusion in the larger companies—in the form of trust agreements—enraged farmers. They lashed out against railroads, banks, and all big industry. In this situation Congress, alert to the political strength of agriculture, passed the Sherman Antitrust Act of 1890—a law destined to become quite controversial—with almost no debate or opposition.

The key sentence in the Sherman Act was the declaration that "Every contract, combination in the form of trust or otherwise, or conspiracy in restraint of trade among the several states, or with foreign nations," was illegal. The act went on to say that "every person who shall monopolize, or attempt to monopolize, or combine or conspire with any other person or persons to monopolize any part of the trade or commerce among the several states, or with foreign nations, shall be deemed guilty of a misdemeanor [since 1974, a felony]. . . ." What the sweeping and undefined terms of the act

Plagued with declining food prices since 1869, farmers joined the Grange to protest unfair business practices and high prices imposed by the railroads and big industry.

could mean would depend on the way they were applied to specific cases by the federal courts. The act had elevated to statutory form ancient rules of common law against acts in restraint of trade and attempts to monopolize. It was unclear, however, whether all restraints of trade were unlawful or if only *injurious* restraints of trade were prohibited. Most of the congressmen who passed the act appeared to have been willing to leave this question and others up to the courts. They had wanted to enact a law so sweeping in its provisions that it would be unenforceable—and hence harmless. Indeed, many in Congress regarded the Sherman Act as a minor measure of appeasement to the farm group.

Despite the hue and cry against the trusts, Congress probably reflected the nation's predominant mood of laissez-faire. Until 1903 Congress was neither willing nor compelled by public opinion to vote the extra funds that would have made

it easy to enforce the antitrust law. Before 1903 the government brought only twenty-three cases under the act. In 1895 the Supreme Court all but made the act a "dead letter" by ruling that it did not apply to manufacturing. The Court made the Sherman Act a law without authority in its ruling that, because manufacturing occurred before goods entered interstate commerce, manufacturing was only incidentally involved with commerce. The Court took a significant step toward reviving the act in 1899, however, when it ruled that the sale and delivery of a product rather than its manufacture constituted the material part of a commercial contract. The Court ruled that a sale for delivery outside the state made the transaction a part of interstate commerce—hence within the jurisdiction of the federal courts.

Merger Movement. The 1899 decision was also important for other reasons. The case, called *Addyston Pipe and Steel Company*, involved price and marketing agreements between the members of a pool of cast-iron pipe manufacturers. When the Supreme Court declared such agreements void, business managers correctly took this to mean that pools and other forms of *loosely knit combinations* would be held illegal under the Sherman Act. They then proceeded incorrectly to assume the obverse—that *closely knit combinations* would be considered legal. Acting on this assumption, they turned with enhanced enthusiasm to a merger movement that was already under way. This movement, which reached its peak around the turn of the century, resulted in the creation of the United States Steel Company, American Tobacco Company, International Harvester Company, Du Pont Company, and many others. Its effects on the U.S. economy were therefore widespread and enduring.

A merger is a combination into a single firm of two or more previously independent enterprises. There are two ways that mergers may occur: through consolidation and through acquisition. In the great turn-of-the-century wave of mergers the consolidation process was used most frequently. Consolidation was required when large sums were necessary, as in the case of U.S. Steel, capitalized at $1.4 billion—the first billion-dollar corporation in American history. Acquisition was used when the cash sum needed was not beyond the capital resources of an existing firm.

The New York Stock Exchange played an important part in facilitating these mergers. New firms brought into being for the purpose of effecting the mergers had been incorporated as holding companies. Often the technique for gaining control of previously independent firms was to exchange holding company stock for a controlling number of shares in operating companies. Promoters were most likely to take steps toward consolidations when stock market values were rising, because the prospects of profitable stock sales served as an attractive inducement to the stockholders in firms to be merged. The state of the stock market was also a consideration when the technique of control involved the purchase of firms for cash (acquisition), since new capital issues were often required to raise the cash.

The need to raise gigantic sums of money brought to the foreground of American business those who specialized in the marketing of securities. In the first two post-Civil War decades of manufacturing growth the financing of firm expansions had largely been carried out by industrialists themselves. Now, in the merger movement of the 1890s, investment bankers like J. P. Morgan had the leading roles. Investment bankers had gained valuable experience in the huge reorganizations of railroad corporations in the 1880s and early 1890s. The marketing of railroad stocks in connection with these reorganizations had developed the New York capital market to the point where it could help finance industrial mergers in the late 1890s.

The prominence of the New York Stock Exchange and of the investment bankers and promoters in the great merger movement strongly suggests that the desire for profits from sales of stocks on a rising market was responsible for the movement. The desire for scale economies (increased efficiency of operation due to greater size) apparently had little to do with it. Except in the primary metals industries, the overwhelming majority of mergers were horizontal in nature rather than vertical. Some of these mergers, nevertheless, did achieve certain scale economies through administrative reorganizations. Profits from sales of stocks were not enough for the industrialists, however. They also sought to protect and enhance profits from sales of goods by controlling the market more tightly and weakening competition. One of the easiest ways to eliminate competition is to buy out competitors. Merging smaller competitors into larger firms enabled the surviving corporations to enjoy a leading and influential position in their respective markets. Between the 1870s and 1905 corporation control of the markets rose markedly.

Investment bankers as well as industrialists wished to protect their profit margins by narrowing competition. Because of the excessive competition among the railroads, the bankers had intervened financially in that field. When they turned in the 1890s to industrial firms, they saw the same threat of small returns and of bankruptcy from cutthroat competition. Unless purchasers of industrial securities were protected from this threat, the investment bankers' own profits from securities sales would be jeopardized. As in the case of railroads, therefore, they insisted that one or more of their representatives have a seat on each corporation's board of directors and that the investment banking house act as fiscal agent for the corporations whose securities it handled. Having representatives on these boards put bankers in a position to veto costly and unwise plans. It also gave them a potentially high degree of control over the operations of the industrial firms. Another result of bankers' control was that they often had a chance to select the firms' chief executive officers.

Investment banking control became highly significant, and during this brief era of "finance capitalism" it extended to the outer edges of the American economy. By acting as fiscal agents for industrial firms, investment bankers became their "depositories," using the sums deposited to invest in their securities businesses generally. To serve the capital needs of the largest corporations, they acquired control of insurance companies and other large securities customers, as well as some sources of credit. Investment bankers purchased controlling shares of stock in insurance companies and commercial banks. They also formed "interlocking directorates" through which virtually the same group of directors could control seemingly unrelated corporations. Thus investment bankers became the pivot of a large area of economic activity. The colorful but somewhat exaggerated report in 1912 of the Pujo Committee of the House of Representatives that followed its investigation of the "money trust" disclosed that

Announcing his bank-control plan, Woodrow Wilson reads the "death warrant" of the money trusts. The disclosure of concentrated financial control in the banking industry led to the enactment of the Federal Reserve Act.

eighteen financial institutions had interlocking directorates with banks, railroads, industrial corporations, and utilities. The institutions controlled 746 directorships in 134 corporations, with total resources of approximately $25 billion. This relevation of concentrated financial control led to the enactment of the Federal Reserve Act in 1913 and also to the prohibition of interlocking directorates by the Clayton Antitrust Act in 1914.

Mergers and Antitrust Enforcement. The great merger wave ebbed during 1903 and 1904. In 1904 the U.S. Supreme Court handed down another major antitrust decision in the *Northern Securities Company* case. The Northern Securities Company had been incorporated as a holding company for the purpose of uniting the Northern Pacific and Great Northern railroads. To the great surprise of the business community, the Court ruled that the acquisition by a holding company of stock control of competing carriers constituted an illegal monopoly. The case had been dramatically pushed by President Theodore Roosevelt, who was known as a "trust-buster," though his ambivalent role in antitrust matters hardly qualified him for the title.

Roosevelt preferred the idea of a Bureau of Corporations, established in 1903, to investigate trusts and publicize abuses. So far as antitrust enforcement was concerned, he refused to molest industrial giants who agreed with his regulatory approach, whereas companies that antagonized him became the subject of vigorous prosecutions. The Standard Oil Company was the most notable example of those that displeased him. In the 1911 Supreme Court decision in the Standard Oil case (and in that of the American Tobacco Company the same year), the Court adopted its famous "rule of reason."

The rule of reason drew a distinction between "reasonable" and "unreasonable" restraints of trade. In the Standard Oil case and the American Tobacco case, the Court inquired into the business behavior of both firms and ordered them dissolved. That the Court had used governmental power under the antitrust laws to dissolve two industrial giants was significant enough: by 1900 American Tobacco was producing from fifty percent to ninety percent of every type of tobacco product except cigars, and in 1906 about ninety-one percent of the refining industry of the country was directly or indirectly controlled by Standard Oil.

Even more significant, however, was the fact that the Court had not based its dissolution order only on the size of the

Theodore Roosevelt launched an attack on the Northern Securities holding company—pushing the case through the lower courts. In 1904 the Supreme Court upheld the lower court rulings—declaring that the combination constituted an illegal monopoly.

Standard Oil, one of the most powerful trusts, controlled most of the refining industry at the beginning of the twentieth century. In 1911 the Supreme Court ordered the dissolution of the industrial giant for practicing "unreasonable" restraints of trade.

firms in relation to their markets. What concerned the Court was not the fact of near monopoly control but the question of whether monopoly had been the *intent* of the companies. It found evidence of such intent in business practices such as railway rate discrimination, local price cutting, and territorial allocation of markets to member companies. These, the Court said, were unreasonable practices. They constituted undue restraints of trade, and the purpose of the Sherman Act was to protect the public from their consequences.

The Court refrained from condemning bigness in itself. If bigness were achieved by fair means, by the practice of superior competitive efficiency, it could hardly be condemned as illegal. Anyone who believed in competitive free enterprise would logically adopt this viewpoint. But logic was not enough. During the opening decade of the twentieth century the "muckrakers" had filled the pages of popular magazines with exposures of the evil deeds of big business. The Supreme Court cases had provided further information. The truth seemed to be that competition was threatened by unfair business practices and that it was these practices that led to monopoly or near monopoly. The way to preserve competition, therefore, was to nip monopoly in the bud by outlawing unfair practices. A deep sense of public misgiving made antitrust policy a major issue in the 1912 presidential campaign. In 1914, under the leadership of the victorious President Woodrow Wilson, Congress responded by passing two new laws in an attempt to strengthen and clarify the Sherman Act.

FTC and Clayton Acts. Declaring that "unfair methods of competition in commerce" were illegal, the Federal Trade Commission (FTC) Act set up a five-person commission to maintain a vigilant watch over the American economy. The act gave the commission the power to investigate the organization, business conduct, and management of any corporation engaged in interstate or foreign commerce, except banks and common carriers. The commission's duties included that of helping to enforce the Clayton Act. The Clayton Act outlawed specific business practices when their "effect . . . may be to substantially lessen competition or tend to create a monopoly." In an effort to prohibit large firms from bankrupting small ones by selling below cost, the act declared price discrimination illegal. It prohibited the use of "tying contracts"—contracts by which firms required their customers to purchase certain commodities as a prerequisite to being supplied with the goods they needed. It forbade competing firms to form interlocking directorates. Finally, it forbade firms to buy stock in other corporations where the effect of the purchase might be to lessen competition.

For all of its exactness, the Clayton Act at first added little to the government's power to enforce competition. It did authorize private parties to sue for injunctive relief against antitrust violators and to sue for treble damages if they were injured by a violation of the antitrust laws. These two innovations later became quite useful in overall antitrust enforcement. During the earlier years of the Clayton Act's existence, however, the courts found it hard to determine when competition was lessened in a relevant market; they interpreted the act in such a way as to open loopholes for clever corporations. For example, firms forbidden to buy stock in competing corporations soon discovered that they could accomplish the same purpose of restricting competition by purchasing a competing firm's assets instead. This loophole persisted until 1950, when the Celler Amendment brought sales and purchases of assets under the act. The Supreme Court continued to adhere to the rule of reason for the most part. But it began to find certain corporation practices so anticompetitive in nature that they were illegal regardless of the justifications offered to support them. Price fixing, illegal in itself, was the most notable among the violations.

Mergers in the 1920s. Encouraged by judicial doctrine and by lax enforcement of the antitrust laws during the prosperous 1920s, corporations engaged in a second merger wave that swept over the U.S. economy between the end of World War I (1918) and 1929. In the latter year alone approximately 1,200 mergers took place. Unlike the first great merger wave, in which combinations had attained very high percentages of the output of their industries, the 1920s wave usually secured much smaller percentages for the merged firms. This was because the mergers took place among the firms that were smaller than the dominant one in the industry. The effect was gradually to lessen the dominant firm's share of an industry's production but to continue the concentration of power in fewer and fewer hands.

Steel, petroleum, agricultural implements, and automobiles were among the industries in which the structure of the market changed from near-monopoly to oligopoly (a situation in which a market is controlled by a few producer-sellers). Some industries that had enjoyed a notable degree of competition, such as dairy products and packaged foods, also emerged with oligopolistic markets. By 1929 corporations were producing more than ninety percent of all manufactured goods, and the two hundred largest corporations were receiving twenty-two percent of the total national income.

Antitrust Enforcement in the 1930s. Under the National Industrial Recovery Act (1933–35), the Sherman Act was virtually suspended. A vigorous program of antitrust enforcement was begun in 1937, however, by Thurman W. Arnold, head of the antitrust division of the Department of Justice. More prosecutions were initiated between 1937 and 1948 than in the entire history of the Sherman Act before 1937.

Actions were brought mainly against established oligopolies, but, although the government won most of the major cases, the penalties were not as harsh as they might have been. Issuing drastic dissolution orders to corporations might have reduced some firms to uneconomic size, and the courts were reluctant to risk that.

Conglomerate Mergers. After World War II, a third merger wave occurred. In the 1951–55 period, the total number of mergers was substantially greater than for any other five-year period in the preceding twenty-five years. Many of these mergers were of a type known as "conglomerate"—the acquisition by one enterprise of another engaged in a noncompetitive field, as a means of diversifying its interests. The diversification movement has probably been the outstanding corporate development of the twentieth century. Although it began in about 1904 and gathered momentum after World War I, it became widespread only after World War II.

Because it turns out many products instead of only one, the typical large corporation has had to work out a more complex administrative structure to replace the simple one used by its recent predecessors. As the corporation moves into new lines of products, a multifunctional unit called a division is set up for each major product line or large geographic area. Each division has a central office that administers a number of departments responsible for a major function, such as manufacturing, sales, finance, or research and development. Each of the departments, in turn, has a departmental headquarters that coordinates, appraises, and makes plans for a number of field units. Field units are at the lowest administrative level of the corporation.

Over all of these administrative levels, at the top of the corporate pyramid, is the general office, where executives and staff specialists coordinate operations, plan goals and policies, and allocate resources to the various divisions. Each division tends to be quasi-autonomous and fairly self-contained.

The people at the top normally have only a very small ownership interest in their enterprises. Ownership of voting stock is so widely scattered among tens of thousands of shareholders, however, that it is extremely difficult for a dissident minority to dislodge a management in power. The effort is not often made, partly for this reason and partly because the great majority of stockholders may be indifferent to management decisions so long as their dividends remain satisfactory. The top executives try to insure their continued control by moving the corporation into new and profitable product lines. The oligopolistic market power of a producer-seller provides insurance against loss from declining prices or uncontrolled production. In addition, management's control of dividend policy provides ample funds for expansion into new areas, into which the corporation may move either through research and development or through the acquisition of other firms.

Pros and Cons of Antitrust Law. Some observers do not regard the large size of the contemporary corporation as a major problem, nor do they consider the antitrust laws to be of great importance. After all, Congress has from time to time specifically exempted from the operation of the antitrust laws such groups as agricultural cooperatives, export trade associations, and labor unions. The Robinson-Patman Act (1936) put a greater emphasis on preserving small business competitors than upon promoting competition, since it prohibits selective price cutting.

Some critics of the antitrust laws, who favor corporation power, point to the existence of a "new competition" in service, in new products and processes, and in advertising; they suggest that such competition fosters consumer interests in ways that the old price competition did not. Some argue that the old competition among sellers on the same side of the market has given way to a "countervailing power" from the other side, with mass buyers and large trade unions arising to share the gains of oligopolistic sellers. Other antitrust critics point to the existence of interindustry competition as the reason that a monopoly in any field would be unable to exploit the public. Still others argue that corporate managers have developed a sense of social responsibility and that private industry can by itself achieve a just balance between the claims on corporate earnings of workers, investors, consumers, suppliers, the local community, and the nation.

On the other side of the question are arguments for the many positive benefits that the antitrust laws offer. For one thing, strict enforcement of the laws breaks up the great economic power of the giant corporation. Excessive concentration of power often prevents efficient distribution of resources and holds back economic growth, once all possible economies of scale have been achieved. Many argue that resources devoted to advertising are largely wasted from the consumer's point of view. Although the separation of ownership from control is as old as the use of the corporate form in business, in the modern setting professional entrepreneurs may use their control of dividend policy to keep earnings in the business in order to finance expansion that may actually be unwise. Corporate decisions to move a huge plant to another area for the sake of tax or other cost advantages may result in the deterioration of older communities. The edge of business creativity may be dulled by the routine of bureaucratic processes.

The enforcement of the antitrust laws by the Justice Department, through criminal proceedings, civil proceedings to enjoin anticompetitive practices, and civil proceedings to prevent or undo anticompetitive mergers, has played a vital role in protecting fair competition and deterring excessive concentration. Equally important have been the private suits brought against alleged antitrust violators. Persons who believe that their businesses have been injured by a competitor's conduct in violation of the antitrust laws may sue for three times the amount of money damages they suffered, as well as for injunctive relief. This provides a strong incentive for private enforcement, and it relieves the Justice Department of some of the burden of ensuring compliance with the laws. In recent years, Congress has strengthened the antitrust laws in several important ways. This indicates that, for the time being, the nation remains committed to the goals of fair competition and deconcentration of power that originally inspired the Sherman Act.

Corporation Law

The twentieth century has seen a movement in corporation law away from rigid formalities and toward greater flexibility in the treatment of certain matters: amendments to the articles of incorporation; actions for which shareholder consent is necessary; restrictions on the ways in which corporate finances must be handled; and transferability of shares. More important than these changes in state corporation law, however, has been the invasion of the field by other statutes that regulate a variety of matters including public offerings of corporate securities, solicitation of proxies in large corporations, accounting methods, security issues, and consolidations of railroads and public utilities. The statutes also establish a national statutory system for the reorganization of insolvent corporations. "Judge-made" business corporation law has also contributed to the flexibility of corporate law since the turn of the century.

There has been a further legislative development with indirect bearing on the law of corporations. Statutes have been enacted that permit partners to sue and be sued and to hold title to property in the partnership name; they can also make agreements for the disposal of partnership interests on the death of any partner so as to preserve the continuity of the business in the survivors, and even elect under certain circumstances to be taxed as a corporation. These statutes have tended to reduce most differences between the two forms of association—corporations and partnerships—particularly when compared to statutes that permit the formation of "close corporations" (those that are small enough to be relieved of many corporate formalities and resemble partnerships in many ways). The only important difference that remains between the two forms of association is the limited liability of shareholders and the unlimited liability of general partners for the business's obligations.

Organization of Stock Corporations. Most business corporations in the United States are organized under a general corporation act of a specific state that provides for the interests of the members to be represented by transferable shares of stock. The act usually authorizes a group of three or more persons to form a corporation by signing and filing in one or more public offices a certificate of incorporation or corporate charter. There is, however, a trend to permit incorporation by a single person.

Among other things, the certificate of incorporation states the number of shares, the rights belonging to each class of shares, and the amount of capital with which the corporation will begin business. Sometimes, however, the certificate authorizes the directors of the corporation to determine what classes of shares will exist and what rights will belong to each class. Before a corporation may effectively take actions in its own name, it must be legally organized.

Powers of the Corporation. The legal powers of a corporation are those given it, expressly or by implication, either by the corporation law or by its charter. In exercising these powers the business corporation functions—to use political terminology—like a representative government. Shareholders elect a board of directors empowered by statute in most of the states to "manage" the business. Typically, the only powers expressly given to shareholders are powers to elect directors, enact bylaws, and approve or disapprove directors' resolutions on important issues.

Where a corporation's board of directors is composed of a large number of persons, it is customary to delegate broad powers to executive or other committees. Many statutes expressly authorize such delegations. Delegation of responsibility to individual officers is a practical necessity; most statutes provide that corporations shall have at least three officers—a president, treasurer, and secretary—without specifying further what functions the officers are to serve.

Normally, in order for an action of the board of directors to be valid, it must be taken at a formally convoked meeting. There has been a recent trend in court decisions, however, to uphold informal action *not* taken at such meetings, especially if all directors know of the action, if the shareholders have acquiesced in it, and if no minority interests are adversely affected. The courts' tolerance for irregularities does not extend to the same degree to action called ultra vires (beyond the corporation's authority) that is either inconsistent with some provision in the certificate of incorporation or is not reasonably related to the purpose of the corporation as stated in the certificate. Few actions are invalidated on the ground that they are ultra vires, because most certificates of incorporation authorize all legitimate business activity and because many states no longer allow the defense of ultra vires in actions between the corporation and outsiders.

Voting Rights and Voting Control. Shareholders have little or nothing to do with the day-to-day management of a business, but they are the ultimate source of authority. Most statutes require an annual meeting of shareholders to be held, at a time usually provided for in the bylaws. Special meetings may be held upon proper notice. The shareholders who have voting shares elect the directors. The consent of the holders of at least a majority of shares (sometimes more) is necessary in order to liquidate a solvent corporation, merge it with another enterprise, or amend the certificate of incorporation. The statutes make it impossible to divest the entire body of shareholders of voting power in these matters. However, most state statutes do permit the creation of a type of share that can be largely stripped of all voting rights. Voting power is usually proportional to share ownership.

Shareholders can vote either in person or by "proxy" (through an authorized representative). Most proxies are mailed to persons who are connected with management after information about the annual meeting has been sent out. But the shareholder may give his proxy to anyone he chooses, as long as the proxy holder attends the meeting. Occasionally, fights for corporate control are conducted by rival groups competing for the shareholders' proxies. Federal law provides that any person who solicits proxies of corporations covered by the law must conform to regulations, issued by the Securities and Exchange Commission, that require full disclosure of material information.

Obligations of Directors and Officers. It is the duty of directors and officers to exercise their powers in the best interest of the corporation. This does not mean that a director or officer can never put himself in a position in which his economic interests are to any extent contrary to those of the corporation. It does mean, however, that any transactions between a director and his corporation will be set aside if the corporation wishes, unless the director is found to have acted with scrupulous fairness. Most courts have held that (unless the certificate of incorporation provides otherwise) a director's contract with his corporation must have the approval of a majority of the disinterested members of the board.

Fairness is hard to define in this connection, but it normally includes a duty of "full disclosure," both of the director's contrary interests and of facts known to him that affect the desirability of the proposed agreement. An alternative test for fairness is to consider whether the proposition submitted would have commended itself to an independent board if the entire board of directors is potentially interested in the transaction.

What is the permissible degree of conflict between the corporation and an officer who in some way stands to make a direct or indirect personal gain from a corporate transaction? The law is uncertain on this point. Directors and officers have a fiduciary duty (one founded on trust) of loyalty to the corporation that requires them to allow it to reap the benefits of any "corporate opportunity" that may be available. In addition to their duty not to allow any decisions that they make as managers to be warped by self-interest, directors owe the further duty of "reasonable care and prudence." Imprudent management by directors is of various kinds. It may result from failure to attend meetings, failure to keep well enough informed about corporate affairs to act intelligently at meetings, failure to supervise or provide for adequate supervision of subordinates, or reckless or incompetent business judgment. On the other hand, the courts in general have not held directors legally liable for simple errors of business judgment.

Extremely important statutory additions have been made to the law governing the conduct of a director who is not acting for the corporation but is purchasing some of its shares from a shareholder. Most of the earlier court decisions in this field permitted a director to buy shares without disclosing any inside information that he might have. The practical effect of the rule was to enable a director, in dealing with individual shareholders, to take advantage of information that he had obtained through the position of trust to which shareholders had elected him. Many courts have repudiated the earlier view and have either required full disclosure in all cases or insisted on it in cases where purchases without full disclosure would be particularly unfair.

Full disclosure of "material information" under all circumstances is required by Section 10 of the Securities Exchange Act of 1934 and Rule 10b-5. This rule was issued by the Securities and Exchange Commission for cases in which the director brings himself within the regulatory powers of Congress by using the mails or another instrument of interstate commerce (such as telephones). Although the language of both the statute and rule is rather vague, the courts have enforced them vigorously and have used them to prohibit almost all fraudulent or intentionally unfair securities transactions by insiders. Other federal statutes provide that, in certain defined situations, an officer, director, or large shareholder who purchases and sells shares within a six-month period is liable to the corporation for any profits earned from the transaction. This latter provision gives no remedy to the seller of the shares; it is designed instead to discourage the practice of short-term market trading by corporate officials.

Legal Obligations of Promoters and Controlling Shareholders. It is possible to promote a corporation and to dominate its original board of directors without becoming, in any formal sense, its official representative. A promoter who organizes a corporation in this manner is in a position to make highly inequitable contracts with the corporation and to obtain large profits that will seriously lessen the value of the securities that the corporation issues to other people. The courts have attempted to cure this evil by obliging the promoter either to permit rescission (cancellation) of the transaction or to surrender his secret profit. Additionally, and far more effectively, the Federal Securities Act of 1933 requires full disclosure of the material details of any new stock distribution.

A majority shareholder or a group of shareholders acting together and constituting a majority can (like a promoter) use their control to make the type of contracts with the corporation that deplete its assets and cause loss to other shareholders. Since shareholders have not, like directors, undertaken to act for the corporation's benefit, they are not subject to all the legal disabilities that apply to directors. Recent cases, however, have begun to impose some duties of fair dealing on majority shareholders. It may now be necessary for them to account to other shareholders for special advantages that they enjoy, such as premiums paid for the privilege of controlling the business.

Shareholders' Suits. Officers, directors, and controlling shareholders would, as a practical matter, often be able to violate their duties to the corporation with impunity (without punishment) if it were not for an invention of courts of equity called "the shareholder's derivative suit." Ordinarily, the power to bring suit on a corporate cause of action is vested in the directors, but they will not exercise that power if they themselves are the wrongdoers. To meet this situation, the courts developed the shareholder's derivative suit, which permits one or more shareholders to sue on a corporate cause of action for the corporation's benefit. This can be done only if the board of directors unreasonably refuses to sue, or if— because the directors are the alleged wrongdoers—they are not proper persons to conduct the litigation. Such suits have often served a very helpful purpose. But they have also led to such serious abuses as losses to the corporation, because of unjustified interference with day-to-day business, and losses from litigation expenses and settlement costs in suits that were brought solely for their nuisance value. Two different kinds of remedies for these evils have been developed. Court approval must be obtained and notice given to all the other shareholders before a suit may be dismissed or a settlement accepted. In addition, the suing shareholder must put up in advance the likely expenses of the litigation, in case the corporate officers are successful. Statutes also limit the right to sue to those who owned shares in a corporation at the time of the acts complained of.

In support of the suing shareholders, on the other hand, are statutes ensuring their access to the books and papers of the corporation at reasonable times and laws guaranteeing shareholders' rights to inspect and copy the list of all shareholders' names and addresses. In addition, most large corporations are required by federal statutes to make periodic public reports of their assets and earnings and, in cases in which proxies are being sought by the management, to furnish financial reports to their shareholders.

Types of Corporate Securities. The principal types of corporate securities are common shares, preferred shares, bonds, and debentures (unsecured bonds). Preferred shares and bonds may be converted into other types of securities, and the corporation may also have warrants outstanding. Warrants are transferable options—either unlimited or limited in time—to purchase shares of the corporation at a specified price. Warrants are usually first attached to bonds or preferred shares, as an added inducement to buy. All corporations have common shares; they may or may not have securities of the other types.

As a general rule all types of securities are transferable—bonds and debentures by mere delivery, preferred and common shares by delivery of the share certificate accompanied by a transfer power. Preferred shares have priority over common shares with respect to dividends at a limited rate. Under some kinds of preferred-share contracts, they can be offered with the common shares in any additional dividends. These shares are usually preferred and limited in their rights to corporate assets in case of dissolution.

New Issues of Shares. If there is no provision to the contrary in the certificate of incorporation, each shareholder has the right to subscribe for a proportionate part of any new issue of the corporation's shares, in order to preserve a proportionate interest in the corporation. This preemptive right does not apply to shares that are issued for property or to so-called treasury shares (shares previously issued and subsequently reacquired by the corporation).

The public sale of new issues of securities that are fraudulent or are offered without sufficient disclosure of essential facts about the enterprise has engaged the attention of state legislatures. Most states have enacted "blue-sky" laws that require licensing of the persons who sell the securities and usually of the securities themselves by some state administrative agency. A few state statutes, including that of New York, instead of requiring licenses for the public sale of securities, authorize the attorney general to investigate fraudulent practices in connection with such sales and to institute injunction proceedings.

The Federal Securities Act of 1933 differs radically from most state laws. Its sole purpose is to compel full disclosure. With limited exceptions, it provides that no corporate security can legally be offered to the public by mail or by means of any instrument of interstate commerce unless the corporation issuing the security has filed with the Securities and Exchange Commission and made public a registration statement containing full information about the security. The issuing corporation must also provide full information about itself. The commission has the power to sue to prevent sale of the securities if no such statement has been filed or if it finds that the statement is in any way false, misleading, or incomplete. Most of the information in the registration statement must be included also in a prospectus (a statement describing the corporation), which must be given to each original purchaser at or before the time the security is delivered.

Shareholders' Individual Liability. Shareholders whose shares are paid for in full are, generally speaking, immune from any other substantial liability for corporate debts, although the laws of some corporations make them personally liable for wage claims in case of corporate insolvency. A sole shareholder, however, or at times a controlling shareholder, has been held to be liable for corporate debts or damages where he or it (if the shareholder is itself a corporation) fails to keep the corporation's business transactions clearly separate from his own and where he gives those with whom he deals the impression that the corporation's debts are his own obligations. It is true that the corporation is treated for most purposes as a legal person separate and distinct from its members. The courts as a rule, however, will not permit a person (or a group) to evade a statute or contract by causing the corporation to do what the statute or contract forbids a person (or a group) to do in an individual capacity.

Dividends and Other Distributions. Corporate assets are distributed by corporations, mainly in the form of dividends. Most corporation statutes restrict the funds available for dividends to surplus or some types of surplus. Some statutes forbid the payment of dividends out of a surplus earned on an increase in the value of fixed assets, such as buildings and machinery. Some statutes greatly restrict the payment of dividends out of a surplus contributed by shareholders as part of the purchase price of their shares. A few state statutes expressly authorize corporations to pay dividends out of current earnings without applying those earnings to eliminate losses carried over from previous periods.

Corporations sometimes purchase their own shares; this is another method by which they may distribute part of their assets to the shareholders. Finally, corporations sometimes distribute dividends in the form of stock instead of cash.

Amendment, Merger, and Consolidation. Shareholders' rights may be radically changed in several ways. One obvious way is by amendment of the corporate charter. Just as important, however, is change through the merger or consolidation of two or more corporations. If each corporation has only one class of shares, the effect of the merger is to modify the individual shareholder's rights only to the extent of making him an investor in a substantially different enterprise.

But if one or more of the corporations has several classes of shares, the merger agreement may provide validly for such changes in class rights as the substitution of common shares of the combined enterprise for preferred shares of the constituent company. Under most merger statutes, however, dissenting shareholders are given the right to withdraw from the enterprise and to be paid the appraisal value of their shares in cash.

Dissolution, Bankruptcy, and Reorganization. A solvent corporation may be dissolved and its business finally settled as a result of the voluntary action of the shareholders. The winding up of an insolvent corporation may be either voluntary or involuntary. The usual procedure for winding up the affairs of insolvent corporations—other than banks, insurance companies, and railroads—is by proceedings in a federal court of bankruptcy.

Insolvency does not always end in liquidation. A corporation may be insolvent, either in the sense of having insufficient current assets to pay its debts as they mature or in the so-called bankruptcy sense of having liabilities that exceed the fair value of its assets. Even though the corporation is insolvent in one of these two ways, it may have a substantial going-concern value. The best or even the only way in which that value can be realized may be through a reorganization in which the assets are not sold to outsiders but the old creditors become the principal or the sole owners of the reorganized company.

Other Types of Business and Private Corporations. The most important types of "nonstock" business corporations in the United States are mutual insurance companies and savings banks. The members of mutual insurance companies are the policyholders. Although most agricultural associations and other cooperative associations are stock corporations, they are usually organized under statutes that narrowly limit the amount of stock any member can hold. There is usually a provision that, after a limited dividend has been paid, any additional earnings shall be divided among the members in proportion to the amount that they have bought or sold through the association.

Statutes of most states contain separate provisions for the organization of religious, charitable, educational, social, and other nonbusiness types of private corporations, which are usually designated collectively as corporations not for profit. These corporations vary in type from small clubs or societies to large educational institutions. Both statutory and judge-made law applicable to such corporations are much less complicated than that applicable to business enterprises. Judges are reluctant to take jurisdiction over controversies relating to their internal affairs, for it is often the case that the controversies are not chiefly disputes about property but about whether the views or actions of some member are compatible with the tenets, objectives, or traditions of the society.

11.
Bankruptcy

"Bankruptcy" describes the status of a debtor who has been declared by the judicial process to be unable to pay his debts. The words *bankruptcy* and *insolvency* are sometimes used interchangeably, but they have distinct legal meanings. *Insolvency*, as used in U.S. courts and in state insolvency laws, means the inability to meet debts as they come due. As defined in the Federal Bankruptcy Act, the term means that the total sum of the debtor's property is insufficient to pay his debts. A debtor thus may be insolvent without becoming legally bankrupt. The converse is also true: a debtor may become legally bankrupt without being insolvent. A bankruptcy adjudication is merely a legal declaration that the debtor has filed a proper voluntary petition for bankruptcy or that creditors have filed a proper involuntary petition against him. The adjudication starts a statutory proceeding for the administration of the debtor's property, which is then taken out of his personal control.

The primary objects of bankruptcy laws are: (1) to obtain justice while not putting undue pressure on debtors; (2) to discriminate between the involuntary inability to meet obligations and the willful refusal or neglect to pay; and (3) to give creditors a fair share of the debtor's assets available for the payment of his liabilities. In modern legislation there has been a fourth object: to foster what might be called a higher tone of commercial morality and to protect the trading community at large from the evils of reckless abuse of credit and unnatural trade competition.

Since creditors have conflicting interests (and are therefore presumed to be incapable of acting together harmoniously), professional trustees and other agents are needed to deal with bankruptcy. Trustees perform both administrative and quasi-judicial duties in return for pay, which comes out of the bankrupt's property.

Background

In the United States the federal and state governments share control over the administration of insolvent estates. The Constitution (Art. I, Sec. 8) gives Congress power to establish "uniform Laws on the subject of Bankruptcies throughout the United States." But the Supreme Court has held that, subject to certain limitations, states also have the power to establish and administer their own bankruptcy or insolvency laws in the absence of any regulation of the subject by Congress. States may also enact insolvency and related laws that do not conflict with any statute that Congress has enacted.

Under its constitutional grant, Congress has enacted four different statutes. The first was passed by the Federalists in 1800 during the John Adams administration. Its repeal in 1803 by the incoming Jeffersonians was an expression of the farmers' view that it favored the merchant class and also of the Republican opposition to the extension of federal powers. The second statute, passed in 1841 during the John Tyler administration, took effect in 1842 and was repealed in 1843—in part as a manifestation of the then-common view that debtor relief was "immoral."

The third statute, a product of the economic crisis that followed the Civil War, was enacted in 1867 and repealed in 1878—partly because of its administrative defects and partly because of creditors' opposition to the new benefits it allowed debtors. The last statute was enacted in 1898 in belated response to the demands for debtor relief that had originated in the panic of 1893. This 1898 law has become a permanent institution. It has been frequently amended (extensively in 1938), but there has been no agitation for its repeal.

All of these statutes and amendments reveal the constant expansion of federal power. The act of 1800 was confined to bankruptcies of merchants and traders. It made no provision for voluntary bankruptcy proceedings and put severe restrictions on discharging the debtor from his obligations. In the 1841 statute, provision was made for voluntary bankruptcy proceedings by nearly all persons. Involuntary proceedings against merchants and traders were retained, and the provisions for discharge were liberalized. The act of 1867 included corporations within its coverage. It made voluntary and involuntary bankruptcy proceedings applicable to traders and nontraders alike, provided for compositions (arrangements to pay made between the bankrupt and his creditors), and made discharge still more easily obtainable. Each of these changes was opposed or contested on constitutional grounds, but each was finally approved or acquiesced in by the Supreme Court.

The present act is more comprehensive than any of its

predecessors. It authorizes proceedings for liquidation of assets for all individuals and for all corporations except municipalities, railroads, insurance companies, banks, and building and loan associations. It provides reorganization or rehabilitation proceedings for the municipalities and railroads that are excluded from its liquidation provisions. The 1898 statute and its amendments offer voluntary liquidation proceedings to all debtors and provide for involuntary liquidation proceedings against all debtors who owe a thousand dollars or more. The only exceptions are farmers, wage earners who earn less than fifteen hundred dollars a year, and such noncommercial enterprises as social, religious, educational, and charitable institutions. Its provisions for discharge and composition are more liberal than those of any previous act.

The most extensive changes appear in the amendments adopted in 1938. Under these amendments, compositions and extensions of payment are authorized for unsecured debts of individual or corporate debtors (Chapter XI of the act); for debts secured by real property (Chapter XII); for all debts of municipalities (Chapter IX); and for all debts of wage earners except those secured by real property (Chapter XIII). Moreover, Section 77 of the act offers a procedure for reorganization to railroads that are engaged in interstate commerce, and Chapter X offers a similar procedure to corporations and to railroads not engaged in interstate commerce. Administration of the insolvencies of national and federal reserve banks is governed by other federal statutes, whereas administration of the insolvencies of insurance companies, building and loan associations, and state banks is handled by state courts or departments.

The state's role in these matters has not developed along neat lines. On the one hand, the Supreme Court has weakened effective state administration of insolvencies in cases where a debtor's business crosses state lines: the Court has ruled that it is necessary to hold proceedings in all states where the debtor has property. On the other hand, the Court has been generous to the states in its rulings on the conflict of state laws with federal statutes. A certain amount of deference is always paid to state court interpretations in this area. In theory, receiverships in state courts are available to all classes of corporations. In practice, however, Chapter X offers a procedure for reorganization that is likely to deprive the state courts of this business.

Liquidation

The sections on liquidation of assets of the Bankruptcy Act are designed to provide an equal distribution of the debtor's assets among his creditors and a discharge of the debtor from his obligations. They set up administrative machinery that is fairly simple. However, they offer rules for administration that are extraordinarily complex. Proceedings are started either by a petition filed by the debtor himself or by a petition filed against the debtor by his creditors. In the latter case, the petition may be filed by three or more creditors whose claims technically total at least five hundred dollars or by a single creditor with claims in the same amount (if there are fewer than twelve creditors in all).

When the petition is involuntary, adjudication does not follow as a matter of course. It will occur only on a showing that the debtor has committed an act of bankruptcy within four months of the filing of the petition. The statute prohibits the following actions, called "acts of bankruptcy":

(1) fraudulently conveying (transferring) the debtor's property to put it beyond the reach of creditors;
(2) making payments that show preference toward some creditors while the debtor is insolvent;
(3) allowing a creditor to obtain a lien by legal proceedings on the debtor's property while the debtor is insolvent;
(4) transferring the debtor's property to an assignee for liquidation for the benefit of creditors;
(5) obtaining or allowing the appointment of a receiver while the debtor is insolvent or unable to pay debts as they mature; and
(6) admitting in writing the inability to pay debts and the willingness to be judged a bankrupt.

A petition for bankruptcy must be filed in the federal district court where the debtor has his principal place of business or, essentially, where he has lived for the previous six months. A voluntary petition operates as an automatic legal decree of bankruptcy. When an involuntary petition is filed, the debtor is given an opportunity to appear. He also has the right to a jury trial on the questions of the commission of acts of bankruptcy and the issue of insolvency. After the hearing, the court makes judgment of bankruptcy or else dismisses the petition. If judgment of bankruptcy is made, the court normally refers the case to a bankruptcy judge (formerly called a referee).

Bankruptcy judges, unlike regular federal judges with life tenure, are appointed for only a fixed term of years. Nevertheless, they enjoy broad judicial and administrative powers over the allowance of claims and the collection of assets. The orders they issue on these matters, however, are always subject to review by the bankruptcy courts.

When a case is referred to him, the bankruptcy judge secures from the debtor a statement of assets and liabilities and calls a meeting of creditors. At this meeting the creditors may elect a trustee. If they fail to do so, a trustee may be appointed by the court or bankruptcy judge.

The trustee is the executive officer whose duty it is to take possession of the property of the bankrupt and to convert it to cash. The trustee's fee is fixed by the court within a statutory maximum. Creditors are given six months after the first creditors' meeting to file formal claims against the estate. Creditors' claims that are proved are allowed, unless the trustee or other creditors object.

In order to facilitate the liquidation, the trustee is given legal title to all of the bankrupt's nonexempt property. The trustee is also given the power to set aside certain acts: liens acquired by judicial proceedings while the debtor was insolvent; preferential debt payments made by the debtor within four months of the filing of the petition; and fraudulent transferences of property made by the debtor within a certain period of time. Finally, the trustee is empowered to take over any assets that may be held by someone who has taken control of them—following the debtor's action of naming his own receiver—within four months of the filing of the petition.

Limitations

The actual process of distributing the debtor's assets does not bring about a completely equal distribution. The Bankruptcy Act sets out five classes of claims that are to be paid in full before any remaining assets are paid to general creditors. These claims, in order of priority, are:

(1) costs of administration and of preserving the estate,

together with certain filing fees and attorneys' fees;

(2) wage claims made by the debtor's employees, not exceeding six hundred dollars each earned within three months before the petition was filed;

(3) costs incurred by creditors in successfully opposing the discharge of the bankrupt or in producing evidence of certain criminal offenses committed during the proceeding;

(4) most taxes that are due to the federal government or to any state or local governments;

(5) debts that have priority under any other federal law and certain claims for rent with a priority under state law.

One limitation from the debtor's point of view is that he is not automatically entitled to a discharge from the claims not covered by the bankruptcy proceeding. If the trustee or creditors do not object and if the bankruptcy court does not ask a federal district attorney to investigate, the discharge is granted. There are several grounds that may be invoked by the trustee, the district attorney, or the creditors to block the discharge. Lethargy on the part of creditors, however, has produced a situation whereby nearly all bankrupt persons—except those who have received a recent discharge or those who are guilty of the most flagrant dishonesty—are granted discharges. The power given the bankruptcy court to request an investigation by the federal district attorney is rarely invoked. The limitation on discharges is thus more apparent than real.

Another limitation from the debtor's point of view is that even though a discharge is granted, all debts are not thereby released. Only certain claims, called "provable claims," are eligible for the bankruptcy proceeding and are thus dischargeable. Because the statute is ambiguous, there has been extended litigation on the question of what a provable claim is. Generally the answer is that contracts arising *before* the petition is filed are provable claims, but that personal injury and property damage claims made *after* the petition is filed are not. The act sets out several provable debts that are exempt from discharge: most federal and state taxes, liability for fraudulent and other intentional acts, alimony and support orders, certain wage claims, and claims of creditors not notified of the proceedings in time to make a claim.

Reorganization

The later amendments to the Bankruptcy Act were designed not to produce liquidation—that is, distribution of the debtor's assets among his creditors—but to permit the debtor to retain control of the assets after the liabilities have been reduced or the time for payment has been extended. This is done by giving the bankruptcy courts the power to confirm any plans agreed to by a majority of the creditors. These amendments are often defended on the ground that creditors receive more in the end from a debtor's future earning power than they do if the debtor's assets are forcibly sold off at sale prices. But as applied to individual debtors and small corporations, the amendments are primarily designed for the relief of distressed debtors.

The amendment of most practical importance is Chapter X, which supplies a procedure for reorganizing all corporations that are subject to a voluntary or involuntary petition in bankruptcy and all railroads that are not engaged in interstate commerce. This procedure has been widely used since its enactment, especially during the past several years and during other periods of economic slump.

12.
Debtor and Creditor

The law of debtor and creditor is much narrower in scope than the literal meaning of the key words suggests. Many other laws have to do with the creation of relationships that could be called debts in the broad sense. Judgments for damages—for example, those arising from personal injury cases such as automobile accidents—can produce creditors and debtors. The specialized law of debtor–creditor, however, does not cover such debt situations but only covers the area of debt collection. A large part of this law covers restraints imposed upon creditors who are attempting to obtain a debtor's assets.

Appropriation

Debtor–creditor law begins not with bad debts but with transactions that are running smoothly. When two parties have entered into a number of credit transactions with each other and one makes a payment, he is entitled to specify to which transaction it applies. If a person owes a secured debt and an unsecured debt, for example, he may elect to pay the secured debt first.

If the debtor does not specify how a payment is to be applied, the creditor is entitled to apply the payment to the unsecured debt. The creditor is even allowed to change his mind: if the debtor gives no instructions, a creditor may apply the payment to an unsecured debt after having first "improvidently" applied it to the secured debt. If neither debtor nor creditor makes a choice among debts, the usual implication of the law is that a payment will be applied to the oldest debts or to debts outstanding.

Setoff

Another aspect of the debtor–creditor relationship is the practice of offsetting debits and credits so as to leave a net balance that is due from one party to another. This feature often fails to operate until a case is tested in a court of law. Individual practices between creditors and debtors may vary. If controversy arises, however, accounting procedures are subordinated to legal rules. A classic example involves the law of landlord and tenant. A tenant who withholds his rent because the landlord fails to repair the premises makes a costly mistake in most jurisdictions: he must sue separately for repairs and may not merely set them off against his rent. Like many other rules in the law of property, the rule is several centuries old. The reason for its existence is long since past; it nevertheless continues in force in many parts of the country.

The law commonly accepts the business practice that when parties have cross claims the debtor–creditor relationship frequently may be dealt with in terms of net balances. For example, since 1898 the Federal Bankruptcy Act has provided for a setoff of mutual debts and credits between the estate of the bankrupt and a creditor having a proper claim. The statute, however, prohibits certain types of manipulation of setoffs.

Collection Law

The law of collections operates only in the relatively small number of credit transactions in which payment is not made within tolerable time limits. After routine efforts at collection have been fruitless, a claim is commonly put into the hands of an attorney or collection agency. In some states the collection task has been made much more difficult by exemption laws. In recent years, because of high-pressure, and even abusive, tactics by collection agents, Congress has enacted a statute regulating the terms of credit (such as limitations on interest rates), the method and manner of collection, and the dissemination of credit information.

Exemptions. "Exemption" is the right of a debtor to retain a portion of his property even when his creditor has successfully sued him to recover money owed. In the nineteenth century the pattern of exemption laws in the United States was comparatively simple. Exemptions were low in the Northeast and high in the South and West. The pattern has become more confusing, partly because of shifts in wealth and partly because many southern and western states introduced exemptions with high monetary limits that have failed to keep up with inflation.

Few exemptions with a monetary limit that dates from the nineteenth century constitute serious impediments to debt collection today. Exemptions of life insurance have been expanding broadly, even to the point of shielding surrender values of insurance policies within reach of the insured through reserving the right to change the beneficiary.

Creditors' Remedies. A creditor, as such, has no rights to a debtor's property or his earnings. Legal action to collect debts is ordinarily directed at acquiring such rights. It is sometimes possible to attach (take into "custody") a debtor's property or to garnish (legally attach) his wages, bank account, or intangible rights against third persons. These procedures are strictly regulated by statute. In the original thirteen states such a practice was common, with the result that a plaintiff could—and still can to a lesser extent—tie up the very resources that a defendant needed to conduct a defense. The influence of the frontier opposed any strengthening of the creditor's hand in the newer states. Attachments against debtors were rare in those areas.

All collection processes are statutory, although some of the interpretations of American courts trace back to the common-law statutes in England before the colonization of this country. Garnishment is generally not sufficiently flexible to meet various collection needs, and the creditor may have to rely upon other statutory or equitable remedies.

Liens by Legal Proceedings. Liens, in the law of debtor and creditor, are rights of the creditor to hold the debtor's property or, more commonly, to prevent its transfer until the debt is paid. Apart from cases in which an alleged debtor contests and defeats an alleged creditor's claim, the effect of a court judgment for a creditor may be considered here. A court may issue a lien upon any real estate of the defendant, preventing the debtor from transferring the property to someone else. In some states further administration action—such as making a public record of the lien—is necessary. In other states lien upon land can be obtained only by attachment or by a court order that empowers an officer to carry out the court's judgment. Some further process is necessary in order to seize personal property. Frequently this is the seizure of the goods by a sheriff and their sale at a public auction. But the creditor is often the only bidder, and he seldom bids more than his claim, plus interests and costs.

The debtor's interests are protected in such circumstances by having an attorney accompany the sheriff at the seizure of the goods. The sheriff is likely to obtain an indemnity (security) bond from the creditor, which protects the creditor against liability in case of a wrongful levy. In some states, there is no lien prior to the actual levy. Any lien may become vulnerable, as in fraud of other creditors, or it may be otherwise lost through undue delay in enforcement. Court orders have become less effective than they were in the days of smaller populations, simpler business, and more tangible property.

Fraudulent Conveyances. Debtors have frequently tried to put their property into friendly hands for their own benefit or to be generous to their family and friends at their creditors' expense. If a debtor is seeking to cover up his property by these transfers or to be generous to those he provides with gifts, rather than to pay his creditors, the creditors may levy the transferred property as if it still belonged to the debtor or bring an action to have the transfer set aside.

Although some courts have held to the contrary, both the clear language and the intent of the so-called statutes of frauds (modeled after a seventeenth-century English law) allow the question of fraud to be tried in a court action to obtain possession after a debtor's property has been sold. The Uniform Fraudulent Conveyance Act, which is law in many states, and the Federal Rules of Civil Procedure, which apply in federal courts, permit a creditor to establish his claim and to attack a fraudulent conveyance in the same proceeding.

Forced sales usually destroy the values of business that are going concerns. When a business has such a value, it may be advantageous to creditors to conserve it by working out a friendly adjustment under which the debtor has an opportunity to discharge his debts, at least in part. The creditors may agree to extend the time of payment. They may also agree to accept a lesser sum in satisfaction of the whole debt; such an agreement is called a *composition*. Creditors' committees are often formed to supervise a debtor's business during an extension of time or a composition agreement.

Receiverships. Sometimes creditors ask to have a receiver appointed to manage the debtor's business or affairs while a creditors' arrangement is being worked out. A receiver, by definition, is a disinterested third party who manages the debtor's concerns and collects revenues that are due the debtor. The purpose of receivership is to prevent mismanagement by the debtor and to shelter the business from destructive claims while the settlement is being completed.

Receivers are sometimes authorized to carry on the business under the protection of a court order; if so, they are subject to the general supervision of the court. Such a receivership may result in a reorganization of the debtor's business, with some readjustment of the ownership as well as the debts. If the business does not prosper under the receiver's management, however, it will probably have to be sold. But if it can be sold as a going concern to another enterprise, it may produce a better price than would a piecemeal sale of assets.

Bankruptcy. The law of bankruptcy has an important bearing on the law of debtor and creditor. Security transactions must be conducted so as to be able to withstand attack in possible bankruptcy proceedings. Since receiverships are acts of bankruptcy, they are conducted under comparable limitations and may be short-lived. Court-approved liens may be nullified if the debtor's assets are less than his liabilities and if bankruptcy proceedings take place within four months. Other transactions may be set aside by the trustee in a bankruptcy proceeding under certain circumstances.

All such possibilities must be weighed when credit is extended and again when the attempts at the collection of debts begin. The shadow cast by the federal Bankruptcy Act may in some instances promote caution in the extension of credit. It may also serve to warn the aggressive creditor that if he destroys the value of the debtor's business by levy, he may not be able to recover what is owed to him. Debtors and creditors who enter into friendly adjustments should take into account the potential operation of the Bankruptcy Act.

Federal Control. Much of the law of debtor and creditor relationships has been dramatically reshaped in the last decade by congressional legislation. The major instrument of change has been the Consumer Credit Protection Act (1968), whose goals are to insure that debtors are thoroughly informed of the terms of their credit, that garnishment is used only in restricted situations, and that information concerning applications for credit and credit rating is not unduly distributed. In addition, the Uniform Consumer Credit Code (UCCC) provides comprehensive regulation of all extensions of consumer credit except simple charge accounts.

The Consumer Credit Protection Act requires full disclosure of the terms and conditions of finance charges in all credit transactions and credit applications. The act also limits the amount of a worker's wages that may be garnished to twenty-five percent of the weekly pay and provides that no worker may be fired solely because he has his wages garnished for a single debt. The act also prohibits extortionate credit transactions. The act is enforced through the Federal Trade Commission (FTC) and by private suits brought by aggrieved debtors.

The effect of the act and the code is to provide the "consumer of credit" with protection of the right to privacy as well as protection against unclear and misleading credit agreements. Underlying both enactments are the assumptions that consumers are likely to attempt to obtain credit even when prudence might dictate otherwise; that to a certain extent this condition is inevitable in a credit economy; that most substantive restrictions on the extension of credit are impracticable even if wise; and that the consumer can best be protected and the industry least impaired by full disclosure of the consequences of the transactions prior to their beginnings.

IV. Law and the Citizen

> "*Laws made by common consent
> must not be trampled on by individuals.*"
> —George Washington

13.
Property and the Law of Obligations

When we speak of the "common law"—that body of law found in court reports of judicial decisions—we are referring, historically at least, to three areas of subject matter: property, tort, and contract. Strictly speaking, even this division is somewhat misleading. The sixteenth-century lawyer, who grew up with what we would be able to understand as a common-law system, spoke only of land law and the law of "wrongs" or obligations. There were no hard and fast divisions between torts (physical injuries such as harm to the person) and breaches of contract (injuries stemming from broken agreements). The whole history of the common law from the sixteenth through the nineteenth century is, in one sense, an effort to separate and identify individual doctrines to cover the two areas. It is ironic, then, that much of the twentieth century has seen a gradual merging of the two areas back into one general law of obligations. While the twentieth-century American lawyer still may speak legitimately in terms of "torts" and "contracts" law, for many purposes the legal scope of the two areas overlaps substantially.

But even before the difference between tort and contract law was important or even real, the English common law had developed a highly sophisticated and complex body of doctrines to govern land. The common law, then, began with the law of property.

Property: Real and Personal

The division of property into "real" and "personal," like so many things in Anglo-American law, can only be explained historically. In early law, property was deemed to be real if the courts would restore to a dispossessed owner the thing itself (the *res*) instead of merely giving compensation for its loss. All interests in land fell within this category, with the exception of leaseholds (property held by lease), which were regarded at first more as contractual rights than as interests in land. Not until the late thirteenth century could a dispossessed leaseholder recover even damages against anyone except his lessor.

By the end of the fifteenth century it was finally decided that the leaseholder might recover the land itself. By then, however, the classification of leaseholds as personal property had become too firmly established for it to be altered. Thus, if today a person dies leaving all his real property to R and all his personal property to P, all leaseholds pass to P instead of to R. The explanation lies in a distinction that ceased to be important more than four centuries ago.

Real Property

The law of real property in all fifty states except Louisiana (whose legal system is based on the French Code Napoléon) was derived principally from the common law of England. For generations American property lawyers relied upon the standard English texts, such as Sir William Blackstone's *Commentaries* in the eighteenth century and Sir Edward Coke's *Coke Upon Littleton* in the seventeenth century. Even after James Kent, an American jurist, wrote his *Commentaries on American Law* (1826–30) and other important U.S. treatises were available, students of property in America continued to use the English textbooks of the day until those books became so cluttered with expositions of the English statutes of the nineteenth and twentieth centuries that they were no longer helpful either as introductions or as guides to U.S. law.

The U.S. law of real property, even though derived from English law, is not uniform from state to state, however. Under the Constitution, jurisdiction over land law lies almost exclusively with the states rather than with the federal government. Conditions, both physical and social, vary greatly from state to state, and problems relating to land have traditionally been thought to be of local rather than national concern. The American Bar Association has sponsored a variety of uniform or model statutes designed to achieve uniformity in a few isolated fields, but these have not usually been adopted. Moreover, there appears to be little sentiment, even among members of the organized bar, in favor of making the law of real property uniform throughout the country.

The history of American property law consists largely of the substitution of modern rules for the ancient feudal rules that should have been abolished, but were not, when feudalism became obsolete. Fortunately, within the last fifty years most of the states have abolished the totally anachronistic rules. It is striking, however, that many such rules lasted well into the twentieth century.

Estates, Conveyancing, and Mortgages. The nature of a person's interest in land is defined by the extent to which he

(1) may use it as he wishes (free from restrictions by a higher private owner) and (2) may transfer it to another. This is the system of estates adopted from the English common law. The system is rather complex and detailed, but there are only two estates in land that are common and worth noting. One is the "fee simple," which carries the greatest number of rights; under it, land is wholly owned and in every respect is freely transferable. The other estate is the "life estate," which has the fewest rights; under it, ownership exists only for the duration of the life of another person and must be surrendered on that person's death. The estate system was historically a convenient way of apportioning one's wealth in varying degrees among others. Now, however, the only common estate is the fee simple. The other customary way of holding an interest in land is the leasehold.

By the time the American colonies were established, deeds in England very largely had supplanted the ancient feudal formalities for conveying real property. In America the rule that a title to land might be transferred by the execution of a deed was established at an early date. The form of the deed that was used might be one that had been developed by English conveyancers, or it might be one that was prescribed by American statute. It might be a warranty deed, which included covenants, or agreements, for a title by which the grantor (the person giving the property) promised to protect the grantee (the person receiving the property) and his successors against title defects. It might also be a quitclaim deed which transferred the grantor's interest without any warranty as to title. Such deeds, whether warranty or quitclaim, began to operate as a modern counterpart of common-law conveyance. Statutes usually required that the deed, if it was to be effective for all purposes, be signed by the grantor, witnessed, and acknowledged before a notary public or other public official.

Mortgages in the United States took the form of a transfer of title either to the creditor or to a trustee for the creditor, subject to a provision that the transfer would be nullified if the debtor should pay his debt as promised. Various statutes have provided protection for the debtor's interests and have lessened the harsh consequences of failing to meet obligations meticulously. During the depression of the 1930s, "moratoria statutes" (laws permitting a delay in payments) were enacted in many states to shield debtors from the hardships caused by the collapse of the economy.

Rights of Enjoyment. In the United States the rules of law that govern the use and development of land are based upon an assumption that the owner should have the fullest possible freedom to use the land as he wishes. Owners are entitled to use the land as they choose without obtaining either consents from neighbors or permits from the state. The owners might let the land remain unused or, if they prefer, even alter or destroy its substance.

Tracts of land are not independent, however. The development of one tract, especially if it is small, may often affect the use and enjoyment of other tracts. If, therefore, owners are to be secure in the privilege of using their land, the power of each must be restrained to the extent that is necessary to ensure that each owner has the most freedom possible. Thus it was established that an owner of land might leave it in its natural state even though this causes harm to others, but that the owner is not privileged to harm others by using it in a careless or negligent manner. In the mid-twentieth century it was also established that owners could not use land in an extremely hazardous way, even if they did so with the greatest possible care.

In addition, it was established that ownership of land did not justify an encroachment, even though it was innocent, on the land of another—whether the encroachment was on the surface, underground, or in the air. This limitation did not mean, as some thought, that all flight over land without the consent of the owner was unlawful. It meant, instead, that such flight at low altitudes was unlawful even though the upper boundary of the air space that must not be invaded could not be fixed precisely.

The owner of land, moreover, might be held accountable even though he has kept within his boundaries and his use has been neither negligent nor hazardous. Owners are required, in addition, to refrain from any use, however carefully it might be conducted, that interferes unreasonably with the enjoyment of neighboring lands. The difficulty inherent in this limitation is that it is so general that it is vague and hence extremely hard to apply fairly.

In some situations the standards of reasonableness are definite. An obstruction of a vista or of the access of air and light to an adjoining tract by buildings erected close to the boundary is held not to be an unreasonable use. On the other hand, an excavation or mining operation that causes the soil of neighboring land to subside is usually deemed to be unreasonable and hence unlawful even though the work has been done very skillfully. In most instances, however, the limitations imposed on the owners of land concerning the use and development of their tracts are extremely vague.

The test of legality is always the "reasonableness" of the particular use. The standard is that of "give and take, live and let live." To apply it requires the difficult adjustment of the interdependent interests of competing owners. Among the factors that must be considered is the character of the neighborhood. A use that might be appropriate in one locality might be unreasonable, and hence unlawful, in another. The application of common-law rules has tended to segregate uses and to impose upon landowners a crude system of zoning.

The owner's privilege of use is also curtailed if the estate, although a fee simple, is limited by a property right that entitles another person either to use the land for a limited purpose (for example, a right-of-way) or requires that the owner refrain from using the land in a particular way (for example, a right of access to daylight through a window). These rights are called easements.

Originally, all such restrictions were confined within narrow limits, but in the second half of the nineteenth century the courts decided that many types of agreements concerning the use of land should bind not only the parties to the agreement but also successors in title (except buyers in good faith, who bought without notice of the limitation). In the twentieth century "covenants," as the agreements are called, were often relied upon in the development of land for residential use to assure prospective purchasers that a wide variety of uses thought to be undesirable would be barred from the area. Sometimes covenants were used in an attempt to keep members of a particular race from moving into an area, but enforcement of these racially restrictive covenants was declared unconstitutional by the Supreme Court in the cases of *Shelley* v. *Kraemer* (1948) and *Barrows* v. *Jackson* (1953).

Social Control of Land. The freedom of an owner to use and develop land may also be limited by the necessity of submitting to the regulation or appropriation of that land for the public good. Under the U.S. system the powers of government agencies are restricted by the provisions of the state and federal constitutions. Apart from those limitations, private property in land is subordinated to the interests of the state.

The owner's enjoyment of land is subject to the power of eminent domain, and the land (or an interest in it) may be

During the twentieth century a growing number of land-use restrictions have been imposed on property owners by local ordinances. Under New York City's Landmarks Preservation Law, any exterior alterations on a designated landmark must meet the approval of the Landmarks Preservation Commission. In the 1978 Supreme Court decision Penn Central Transportation Co. v. New York City, *the Court upheld the commission's right to prevent the owner of Grand Central Terminal, a building with landmark status, from developing the air rights above the terminal.*

taken away so that it can be used for a project of which the owner does not necessarily approve—such as a highway or an airport. The appropriation must be authorized by a statute that satisfies various requirements, primarily (1) that the appropriation is for a public use, and (2) that the owner is paid a just compensation for the interest which is taken away.

The owner of land is also required to submit to regulations. Even though a loss that the regulations cause an owner is large, he does not have a right to be compensated for the sacrifice made for the benefit of the public. Thus, in *Miller* v. *Schoene* (1928), the Supreme Court held that a Virginia landowner who was required to destroy his cedar trees to protect apple orchards in the vicinity was not entitled to be reimbursed either for the value of the trees or for the consequent depreciation in the value of his land.

In earlier periods, the typical police regulations affecting the use of land were building codes and other regulations intended to protect the health and safety of those who lived in cities. At one time it was doubtful whether such regulations might be applied to existing structures. That doubt was resolved in favor of the power to regulate by the New York Court of Appeals in a landmark case in 1895.

In the twentieth century the scope of regulations imposed upon owners of land has been vastly extended. In the case of *Village of Euclid* v. *Ambler Realty Co.* (1926) the Supreme Court upheld the power of the states to classify communities into zones and to impose different regulations as to use within the various zones (such as residential, commercial, industrial, and so on). Planning commissions were established to formulate programs for community development, and their policies were put into effect by the enactment of comprehensive zoning and subdivision ordinances regulating many aspects of the use of land in metropolitan areas.

In most instances, the courts have insisted that these regulations be justified by a showing that they are reasonably related to the protection of the health, safety, and morals of the public. Often such regulations have been held to be unenforceable because such a showing could not be made. Frequently regulations have been justified on the ground that they have an important relationship to the maintenance by the community of various public services such as streets, schools, fire protection, and sewage disposal systems. The Supreme Court has even held recently that communities may use restrictive zoning laws to control the concentration of so-called adult bookstores. But the Court has stopped short of allowing a municipality to ban extended "families" that are not typical family units from living together simply because the community wishes to discourage population density in certain areas. Zoning laws thus implicate numerous types of constitutional questions.

Efforts to justify land-use restrictions upon purely aesthetic grounds have generally been rejected by the courts. But the fact that the enforcement of regulations would enhance the attractiveness of an area has often been noted by the judges upholding these restrictions. Zoning laws and other forms of regulations are now being used increasingly for environmental purposes. For example, some cities are attempting to create a "greenbelt" area between urban development and nearby scenic areas to prevent those areas from being marred.

Zoning laws have been sharply criticized as devices for restricting access to certain residential areas for persons without enough income to afford the minimum type of housing allowed. Some state courts have accepted this view in a few cases. What is perhaps most remarkable about zoning laws is their adaptability at different times to different goals of urban land-use planning.

Personal Property

Personal property embraces almost anything in existence, other than real property, that is capable of being enjoyed or used. Thus, electric current is tangible property—although invisible and not safely felt—because it is capable of being manufactured, measured, and used. It is often said that there is no property in air or water, yet compressed air or bottled water is certainly property.

Buying or Selling. Ownership of personal chattels may be acquired, lost, transferred, or affected in various ways. One method is by buying or selling. If A wants to buy an automobile from B, A may either: (1) buy it outright for cash; (2) exchange other goods for it (barter); (3) buy it by absolute sale but on credit; (4) take it under a "lease" (bailment agreement) containing an option to purchase on the completion of a certain number of rental payments; (5) buy it under an installment credit plan, similar to the previous method; (6) buy it "subject to return," a sale with the added privilege for A of calling off the sale within a specified time period if not satisfied; or (7) buy it "on approval," a bailment with an option to buy that becomes a sale only if the goods are expressly

The law of property is divided into real property and personal property. Personal property, covering almost anything in existence other than real property, may be acquired or transferred by various means—including barter, buying outright for cash, and buying on credit.

accepted or not returned within a specified time period. Ownership may also change through involuntary sales, including judicial sales, tax sales, and foreclosures of liens.

If the seller was neither the owner nor one who had authority from the owner to sell, or was selling stolen goods, the question arises whether the good-faith purchaser acquires a good title against the unconsenting true owner. Anglo-American law usually protects the unconsenting true owner, with some exceptions.

Gifts. American law restricts the meaning of *gifts* to "gratuitous transfer of personal chattels taking effect on delivery in the lifetime of the donor." Such gifts are divided into two categories: (1) gifts *inter vivos*, those between living persons; and (2) gifts *causa mortis*, those given in case of death.

The principal difference between the two categories is that gifts *causa mortis* are revocable. Moreover, they are automatically void if the donor survives the peril from which he envisaged death at the time the gift was made.

Bailment. Apart from transactions involving transfer of ownership, the most important legal relationship regarding personal property is termed bailment. A bailment arises in almost any situation in which one person (called the bailee) lawfully has possession of the goods of another (the bailor). The indispensable element of a bailment is possession by the bailee. If a repairman comes to a house to repair a clock, he is not a bailee; if the owner leaves the clock at the repair shop, a bailment exists. Railroads, moving companies, and other common carriers are bailees of the goods entrusted to them for shipment. To lessen income taxes and to reduce the amount of capital they must invest, countless companies have become the bailees rather than the purchasers of automobiles, ships, machinery, or equipment.

Although bailments may arise without either a written agreement or a contract, they usually involve a formal written lease (so-called by analogy to a lease of land, but the transaction remains a bailment). Many clauses in such instruments are directly copied from written leases of land. In many instances, therefore, litigation involving such bailment agreements is decided by analogy with the corresponding rule in leases of land. In some jurisdictions certain bailment clauses are unenforceable as being against public policy; other clauses will be enforced, but only if specifically agreed to, and even then they will be narrowly construed by the courts. Agree-

The pawnbroking business utilizes a specialized type of bailment, the pledge. The pawnbroker, or bailee, advances loans to customers who have pledged personal effects as security on the loans.

ments freeing a bailee from liability for his negligence illustrate both of these situations. One specialized type of bailment is known as a pledge. It gives the bailee a lien on goods as security for a loan. The borrower pledges to pay within a time limit. Pledges are used in pawnbroking.

Torts

The word *tort* derives from the medieval French word for "a wrong" or "a wrongful act." A tort is, in effect, a civil wrong for which the law provides relief. It is a shorthand term for a multitude of situations for which a legal action for damages, and frequently equitable relief, may be maintained on behalf of an injured party. The term is usually contrasted with *contract* and *crime*, although many contracts and most crimes may be the basis of tort actions. Tort law has a broad range that is exceedingly difficult to classify. It protects the interests of personality, property, and relations against physical, appropriational, and defamatory harms of many types. Its chief remedy is money damages—actual or punitive—but a tort may also be settled by a court injunction, rescission (the cancellation of a contract), or restitution (the return of things to the status quo with or without compensation).

Tort law in the United States operates through court actions for trespass, nuisance, ultrahazardous risks, negligence, conversion, deceit, slander and libel, privacy, interference with trade or employment, and abuse of governmental power and process. It is primarily "courthouse," or "litigation," law. Of all the areas of American law it is the least controlled by the principle of *stare decisis* (that of following rules laid down in previous judicial decisions). As precedents, tort decisions have high value as arguments in analogous cases. The situations that arise are infinitely variable, however, and these differences are reflected almost unnoticeably by the reactions of court and jury in a particular case. Tort law is thus always in the making, with the scope of its actions being constantly extended or modified. What has been developed by the courts is a process of litigation adaptable to any case that may arise, with parties, witnesses, lawyers, jurors, and judges—sometimes a succession of judges—each exercising an influence in the composite judgment. That judgment binds the parties to the litigation and also provides the basis of argument in the next case, but only with whatever binding effect the particular court may give it. It is the processes of modern tort law that are of primary significance.

Negligence. The basis for negligence is primarily to give protection against unintended physical harm to persons and to property. Many cases that could be tried under other categories of tort law may with little difficulty be translated into cases of negligence—the failure, in view of the danger, to use reasonable care under all the circumstances of the situation. The laws on negligence pertain to injuries arising out of the operations of railway, highway, waterway, and skyway traffic and the activities of public utilities, construction projects, manufacturers, hospitals, landowners, and medical and professional personnel, as well as many other institutions and professions.

The extreme flexibility of negligence doctrine permits a plaintiff to present all pertinent facts and arguments in his support and permits a defendant to offer all relevant data and arguments in defense. In the United States, but not in England, this action requires jury participation and gives wide play for resourcefulness, advocacy, and compromise, whether the case is tried by a judge and jury or by a judge alone. Its doctrines are more extravagant, more comprehensive, and more resilient than those of any other tort action. Although damages are the only remedy, the various amounts assessed provide very flexible means of limiting liability.

Libel and Slander. Historically, the main purpose of laws against slander (oral defamation) was the protection of a person in employment and in community and political relations. Slander was narrowly defined and has since lost most of its importance, except when the scandalmonger goes so far in his charges that he interferes with the victim's profession or employment. The action is highly technical, seldom instituted, and rarely successful.

Civil court action against libel (written defamation) developed out of the common-law action for defamation and the criminal action against libel. But court action against spoken words came to be known as *slander*, whereas the action for defamatory writing and publications came to be known as *libel*.

Libel law has had a peculiar development. It began as a means of suppression and censorship to protect the government against the press. But it has come to be a basic support of free speech and a free press, although the cost of vindicating those rights is sometimes staggeringly high. In early libel law there were no immunities—not even the truth. Gradually immunities developed and grew in number and scope.

Three great areas of immunities restrict libel law so much that its effective value is primarily that of a threat. Thus many libel suits are "nuisance litigation"—suits that are started at most with an eye to lucrative settlement rather than trial, or, more commonly, with the intention of forcing the other side to spend large sums in defense of an action that will be dropped eventually anyway.

One great immunity to libel law is that of public officials, who have complete immunity for what they say or write, even if it is only vaguely incidental to their official functions. Second, the instruments of publication (publishing companies, newspapers, radio, television, and educational institutions, and their many editors, writers, commentators, critics, reporters, and so on) have almost complete immunity for reporting and printing the substantial truth of any public and many private affairs. They also have immunity for publishing any full and fair report or comment upon any public statement, action, or proceeding. Third, the communication of a matter of common interest, however false or hurtful, among members of the numerous business, political, professional, religious, educational, cultural, fraternal, and other groups of our society, concerning any member of the group or any outsider, is immune from libel action unless it is malicious. The burden of proving malice is on the victim.

In brief, it can be said that liability is the exception from the many immunities for defamatory publications that have become "rights," which support the freedoms of speech and of the press. The individual who cannot claim an immunity of some sort is rare, but even then his liability is likely to be negligible unless he falsely charges his victim with crime, dishonesty, or professional disability. The damages awarded in the United States, although they may be heavy in extreme cases, are mostly moderate. Appellate courts frequently scale down the judgments of trial courts. Libel actions in the United States are the most difficult of tort actions to maintain. Most of them are unsuccessful.

Modern Tort Law. The most dramatic development in the law of torts since World War II has been liability for defective products. Indeed, "products liability" has become a great weapon in the hands of consumers who have been injured by products such as exploding soft drink bottles or unsafe lawn mowers. With the California Supreme Court leading the way, under its chief justice Roger J. Traynor, American courts have developed doctrines that hold manufacturers liable for injuries resulting from the normal use of dangerous products, no matter how careful the makers are in producing them. The doctrine is called "strict liability," because the defendant manufacturer is liable even though he may have exercised reasonable care in his activities (and thus could successfully defend himself in an ordinary negligence action). The reason for such liability is twofold: (1) even with reasonable care, some products are so hazardous that a higher standard is required, and the manufacturer is best able to bear the burden of safety; and (2) the manufacturer is also best able to distribute the cost of the risk (that is, the costs of very high safety standards of manufacturing can be spread over a market of thousands of potential buyers). Manufacturers have been highly critical of the development, because, even with higher safety standards, a single defective product can result in a devastating damage judgment for a company.

In a sense the development of products liability reflects a growing concern that the law of torts is so full of peculiarities and tends so much to concentrate only on the case at hand that it cannot deal adequately with the myriad of risks in daily life. The unpredictability of lawsuits and their scattered re-

After several serious and fatal accidents involving the Ford Pinto in rear-end collisions, lawsuits were filed against Ford Motor Company accusing the company of negligence in designing the car. In the law of torts, American courts have held manufacturers liable for the safety of their products.

sults make sound business predictions extemely difficult. One response has been the growth of insurance and, to a high degree, the law of torts, with its kaleidoscope of doctrines, is being replaced by insurance. In many cases, insurance or other compensation programs have already replaced tort law. For example, workmen's compensation plans replaced the pro-employer law of master and servant at the turn of the century. And in many jurisdictions today no-fault auto insurance has replaced the sideshow of personal injury litigation. Insurance does, in an extremely methodical and scientific way, what the law of torts apparently was designed to do after the fact—compensate injured persons on the basis of who should bear the risk. The only real difference is that the question of risk bearing has been shifted under insurance plans from those at fault to those, collectively, with the ability to pay.

Right of Privacy. Court action against the violation of the right of privacy is a recent development of American tort law. In one aspect invasion of the right of privacy resembles libel; in another it may be confused with the abuse of power by police officials. In the strict cases involving the invasion of a person's peace of mind or solitude, it is frequently nothing more than an extension of trespass—either personal assault or trespass upon the victim's premises by eavesdropping or "bugging" his house or office.

The right of privacy is generally said to be the "right to be let alone." But there is no such right, strictly speaking, in a group society. It is rather a right not to be disturbed emotionally by conduct designed to subject a person to great tensions by baring one's intimate life and affairs to public view. Examples are the excessive harassments by loan sharks and collection agencies to force payment of a debt, the tapping of one's telephone, or humiliating and annoying invasions of one's solitude.

Court actions against invasion of privacy have been used chiefly so far to protect people against having someone appropriate some phase of their personalities—such as a likeness, creative art, history, name, or status—for purposes of advertising or other commercial use. In this sense it is the value of publicity or the "right of publicity" that is at issue—the opposite of privacy. In New York this right is protected by statute as a "civil right." It is distinguished there and elsewhere from the exposure of a victim's private life for news or for cultural or educational purposes. Indeed, the Supreme

Court has held that any information—no matter how private or humiliating—produced at a public court proceeding may be published and is protected from privacy suits by the freedom of the press. In privacy cases courts may award damages or issue an order that invasions of privacy cease.

Contracts

The simplest definition of a contract is that it is a promise enforceable by law. If the promise is broken, the remedy sometimes is the specific or actual performance of what was promised, but usually the remedy takes the form of compensatory damages. A usual requirement of a contractual promise is that it be the product of a bargain. That is, the person to whom the promise is made (the promisee) must give the person making the promise (the promisor) something in exchange for the promise. The thing given in exchange (called a "consideration") may be an act—such as the payment of money, the performance of services, the transfer of real or personal property, a forbearance to act, or the making of a return promise of any of these things. Hence, a contract may involve a promise on one side only, or it may consist of a promise in exchange for a promise.

Since a contract is usually a type of bargain, the making of a contract requires the common assent of two or more persons. This means ordinarily that there must be an "offer" by one person and an "acceptance" by the other. An offer is a demonstration of an intention to be legally bound on the basis of stated terms, and an acceptance is assent to those terms.

Other requirements of a contract are: (1) an intent to be legally bound by the agreement (as contrasted with informal family arrangements, for example); (2) reasonably specific terms of performance; and (3) capacity (for example, neither party should be legally too young or mentally incapacitated). Sometimes the parties may add a provision agreeing on the damages to be paid in the event the contract is broken.

Business and social pressures, such as the fear of losing goodwill or credit standing, probably provide the strongest inducements for persons to perform the promises they make. Nevertheless, the enforcement of contracts is generally considered one of the most important functions of the courts, and there can be no doubt that in performing this role the courts contribute to the stability of commercial transactions.

History. Modern contract law is usually traced to the sixteenth-century English practice in the case in assumpsit (an action to recover damages for breaking an agreement). A good deal of the language used in such cases and many of the situations covered are suggestive of modern contracts, but the actual relation between the two is little more than superficial. In any technical sense, there was no law of contract until the nineteenth century. To be sure, there were clear antecedents much earlier, and there were doctrines governing commercial transactions in the marketplace. But there was no coherent body of law or underlying legal theory on contracts until the mid-nineteenth century. Shortly after the Civil War, the law of contract was highly organized and rationalized by American textbook writers, who gave it a unity and uniqueness it had never before known.

Over the next fifty years the law of contract became more sophisticated and more highly technical. There is no doubt that its careful detail may have proved its undoing. During the 1920s contract law became so technical as to be arid and divorced from commercial reality. The problem was that courts and scholars were determined to apply rigidly the rules of offer and acceptance and other technical doctrines, such as consideration, to a highly changeable marketplace. Because such artificial rules were so out of place, imaginative judges—such as Chief Judge Benjamin N. Cardozo of the New York Court of Appeals (later, 1932–38, on the Supreme Court)—and scholars—such as Arthur L. Corbin of Yale University—came up with more flexible alternatives. The model developed principally by Cardozo and Corbin was called, among other things, *promissory estoppel*; it emphasized the fact of reliance by one party on the promises of the other party as the touchstone of liability. Thus, if A promised to do some act, and B—relying on that promise—undertook a certain course of action, B would be able to recover damages from A if A failed to perform and B suffered a loss as a result.

The virtue of the doctrine was that it was both flexible and attuned to the realities of the marketplace. Its vice was that it made the practice of the marketplace the yardstick of acceptable behavior and that it required a detailed factual inquiry into the "reasonableness" of the reliance. Nevertheless, the doctrine was widely accepted, even though limited by statutory enactment and by codification—such as the Uniform Commercial Code.

Indeed, the Uniform Commercial Code, which has been

adopted by every state except Louisiana, has become the basis of modern contract law in the area of the sale of goods. Other contractual relationships are governed by common law and by different statutes from state to state. With the pervasive coverage of modern statutory law, the highly developed nineteenth-century law of contract has been replaced.

One striking feature of contract law in the twentieth century has been the rejection of the doctrine of "freedom of contract." In the late nineteenth and early twentieth century, contracts requiring employees to work long hours for low pay were defended as manifestations of "freedom of contract." During the last fifty years, however, there has been a growing awareness that the fixing of rights and duties by unrestricted private bargaining leads to the oppression of persons in weak economic positions. Judicial decisions have extended some protection to individuals against the pressures inherent in the use of standard contracts by business firms, but the protection has been limited and incomplete. The only real protection has been in statutes governing the use of certain standard contracts, such as the extension of credit and the landlord-tenant relationship. But these statutes and ordinances vary widely from state to state, and the law has yet to deal with the problem across the boards.

Interpretation. Most of the court cases in which a remedy is sought for breach of contract are concerned with the meaning to be attached to the verbal expressions and acts of parties in their dealings with one another. The process of arriving at such meaning is referred to as "interpretation," or "construction." Although these words are for the most part used interchangeably, the latter is perhaps a more appropriate name for the process of determining the meaning of contractual terms on the basis of the total setting of the agreement. Issues of construction arise, for example, in determining whether the parties ever reached an agreement at all and to what extent they are committed under the agreement.

During the first third of the twentieth century, contracts were interpreted quite literally, and words themselves were generally taken more seriously than were their probable meanings. But with the advent of the Uniform Commercial Code, contracts have come to be more liberally construed by the courts in order to enforce the probable intent of the parties.

Remedies. Although the law of contracts includes a number of doctrines covering the performance of obligations, the most important branch of the law is remedies, particularly damages. When one party fails without excuse to perform according to the terms of a contract, the aggrieved party may have a number of remedies, depending on the circumstances. If he himself has fully performed under the contract, he is entitled to a money judgment for any compensation lost. If the breach occurred before the performance by the aggrieved party was complete, as in the case of an employee wrongfully discharged before the end of an agreed period of employment, he is entitled to a judgment for the damages that were foreseeable when the contract was made. The aggrieved party, instead of seeking damages, may elect to bring a suit for restitution—which is the value of the performance he has rendered to the extent that it exceeds the compensation that he has already received. Another remedy, infrequently available in practice, is "specific performance," a court order requiring the defaulting party to perform his part of the contract on the threat of contempt of court.

A Law of Obligations? The divisions between the law of torts and the law of contracts are gradually becoming less distinct. In a sense, the law of contract has been reabsorbed into the law of tort with the result that there is, realistically speaking, a general law of obligations. Leases provide perhaps the best example of the phenomenon. Strictly speaking, of course, a lease is a contract to provide premises in return for a fixed sum (rent) for a fixed period. But the law of leaseholds is governed to a large extent by rules and statutes covering the law of property. On the other hand, the breach of certain terms of the lease will most likely be governed by the statutes or ordinances that fix liabilities and remedies, not by general principles covering contracts. In effect, the statutes governing leases generally proceed on the basis of fault liability, very much like the law of torts.

It is somewhat artificial, of course, to divide the law into large categories such as contract or tort. To the extent that it is helpful to do so, it is also necessary to note when the categories begin to disappear. Perhaps the most convincing evidence of the gradual blending together of contract and tort liability is the near identity, in practical terms, of the remedies for each.

14.
The Law of Wills

A will or testament is the legal transaction by which an owner of property disposes of his assets in the event of death. The terms are also applied to the written document in which the disposal is expressed. Although in modern usage the words *will* and *testament* are interchangeable, until the nineteenth century in Anglo-American law *will* referred to the disposition of real property, and *testament* referred to the disposition of personal property.

In the United States the freedom to dispose of property by a will is regarded as an essential element of individual freedom in general. The power of an owner of property to determine who will have it upon his death is thought to stimulate economic activity. It is also regarded as important that a property owner can modify the rigid rules of descent and distribution of the intestacy laws (which govern situations in which a person dies without a will) so as to adapt them to the situation of a particular family. For example, the owner may wish to leave property to a crippled child, in preference to another child who has the power to take care of himself. Although it is true that the freedom to disinherit a child may be used to induce obedience, the same freedom may also make provisions for charity. The possibility of abuse for reasons of spite, arbitrariness, or whimsy is the price society has to pay for such freedom. In England and the British Commonwealth countries the modern tendency has been for legislatures to give the courts vast discretionary powers to vary such dispositions.

Limits on Freedom of Testation

Freedom of testation (the right to dispose of assets through a will) never has been absolutely unlimited. Nowhere is a provision of a will valid if its enforcement would be shocking to public morals. If a gift is conditional upon an act of the beneficiary that should not be required, the gift is either invalid or valid unconditionally—as for instance, a gift conditional on the beneficiary's changing his religion. Property given a by testament usually cannot be tied up by the testator for an indefinite future. A testator may leave property to a person for life and upon that person's death to someone else. Under the rule against perpetuities, however, the last portion of the bequest must come into operation within, roughly speaking, one generation after the testator's death. This rule is one of the most complicated in the common law, largely because of its rigidity and partly because of the ingenuity of lawyers who attempt to circumvent it. Much of its complexity has been reduced by statutory amendment in recent years, in both England and the United States.

A testator's freedom to disinherit his surviving spouse, children, or other heirs was extensive in ancient Rome. It has also been more extensive in modern Anglo-American law than in the modern civil-law countries, but it has never been without any limits at all. In the United States the surviving spouse is protected against complete disinheritance in every state. As for land, the interests of dower or curtesy (those portions of property to which a widower or widow is entitled by law from the other's estate) have been preserved in one form or another in a majority of the states. Under this system, each spouse has an "estate" in the lands of the other, a portion of which continues beyond the death of one spouse until the death of the surviving spouse. The survivor cannot be deprived of such property without consent by will or by sale, gift, mortgage, or any other kind of transaction. Under the system of the "indefeasible share," the surviving spouse cannot be completely disinherited but is not protected against the other spouse's giving away or using up the property before death.

In most states the two systems are combined, but New York and other states in the eastern part of the country—as well as a few others—followed the example of England and abolished dower and curtesy. The reason was that their existence makes it necessary in every purchase of land to investigate whether the title may not be encumbered with dower and curtesy rights that are not readily discoverable from the deeds.

In jurisdictions that adopted the so-called community property system (Louisiana, Texas, New Mexico, Arizona, California, Washington, Idaho, Nevada, and Puerto Rico), a share in the family wealth is guaranteed to the surviving spouse, who is entitled to one-half of the community property. Such property usually consists of the property acquired during the marriage by the gainful activities of either spouse. Protection of the surviving spouse can, furthermore, be achieved through homestead laws and by those laws that guarantee to the widow (or, frequently now, to either surviving spouse) an income payable out of the estate for a few months immediately following the death of the other spouse.

Formalities of Wills

In order to secure proof, to impress the testator with the importance of the transaction, and to prevent fraud and forgery, a will must usually be declared in writing. A "nuncupative" (orally declared) will is admitted in some jurisdictions as an exception in emergency situations such as those of a soldier on active war duty, a sailor on board a ship, or a person who finds himself in immediate danger of death.

In their rules establishing the requirements for the execution of wills, modern legal systems usually follow one or more of three forms: (1) the witnessed will as developed in England, especially through the "Statute of Frauds" (1677); (2) the unwitnessed "holographic" will (that is, in the testator's handwriting) as developed in French customary law; (3) the notarial will as developed in the late Roman empire. Under the system of the witnessed will, prevailing throughout the United States and in all common-law parts of the British Commonwealth, the instrument may be typed or printed or written by anyone. It must be signed by the testator, and the signature must be attested by two (and sometimes three) witnesses who must also sign their names. Under the system of holographic wills, available not only in most civil-law countries but also in many southern and western states, the entire instrument must be exclusively in the testator's own handwriting and must also be signed by him; witnesses are not necessary. The notarial will, available in most civil-law countries, is dictated by the testator to a notary or simply given to the notary as a public record of the testator's wishes. (Notaries in civil-law countries, not the United States, must be lawyers. They practice estate planning, draftsmanship of wills, and conveyancing.)

Drafting. The proper drafting of a will can be difficult. The U.S. law is complicated not only by its diversity from state to state but also by the fact that, unless the different provisions have been expressly set out in the will, various rules, many of them obsolete, apply. The problems include: (1) how to apportion the burden of death taxes among the beneficiaries; (2) in which order creditors ought to be paid; (3) which assets are to be used for payment of debts; (4) which gifts (legacies) are to be canceled in case the estate cannot pay for them in full;

and (5) what to do when a beneficiary has died before the testator.

Unless the testator has given special powers to the executor (the person named in the will to carry out its provisions), it will be necessary for the executor, in administering the will, to observe cumbersome and expensive formalities. In the United States a will thus tends to be lengthy and complicated, and it appears unwise ever to draft one without expert legal advice. In order to keep up with the changing circumstances of the testator's family and property, and with frequent changes in tax laws, it is advisable for a testator to have the will regularly checked by a lawyer.

Invalidity. A will is not valid if at the time it was made the testator was mentally incompetent or acted under "undue influence" (that is, coercion or fraud). It is difficult, however, to break a will upon any such ground. In the case of an attack on the will on the ground of incompetency, the courts demand strict proof that the testator, when he made the provision, was mentally unable to know what he owned or who were his relatives, or that he was unable to form a reasonable plan for the disposition of his property. In short, the courts tend strongly toward upholding a will's validity, and the casebooks are dotted with examples of testators with mercurial eccentricities whose wills were upheld against challenge. Thus, the mere fact that the testator labored under some insane delusion does not affect the validity of his will unless it is proved that the delusion actually constituted the motive for the disposition he made. Coaxing and persuasion are generally not held to constitute undue influence unless there were actual threats. A testator may be led, but he may not be pushed. Undue influence may be held to exist, however, if a will was brought about by a person upon whom the testator was dependent or whom he was likely to obey blindly.

The statutory formalities prescribed for execution of a will must be observed meticulously. An unwitnessed holographic will may fail because the instrument contains a printed letterhead or some other words, figures, or signs in print, a rubber stamp, or another person's handwriting. A witnessed will may fail because a witness signed it outside the testator's line of sight, because the witnesses were not told that the instrument was the testator's will, or because a blank space was left between the end of the text and the signature of the testator. The witnesses should be absolutely disinterested parties, that is, persons who derive no direct or indirect benefits from any provisions of the will. A witness may be held to benefit indirectly, for example, if his wife is appointed in the will as executor and thus given the opportunity to earn the fees of that office. Ordinarily, attestation of a will by such a disqualified witness will not result, however, in the invalidity of the entire instrument but only of the provision from which the witness would have benefited.

Revocation. A will is said to be "ambulatory"—that is, it is of no effect until the testator's death. It can be revoked or changed by him at any time. Revocation is accomplished either by the testator's physically destroying the will or by his executing a new will whose provisions are incompatible with those of the earlier one or which provides simply that the earlier one is revoked.

In many states a will is also revoked automatically if the testator marries after its execution. In Anglo-American law, a will remains revocable even if the testator has promised that he will not revoke it; but if he does revoke a will, his estate will be treated as if the testator had lived up to his promise.

Probate and Administration

In common-law countries, it is usual for the testator in his will not only to direct who is to have his property and under what terms but also to appoint an executor by whom the estate is to be settled. If no executor has been appointed in the will, or if the person appointed is unqualified or unwilling to serve, an administrator will be appointed by the court to carry out the terms of the will.

In the United States a will cannot be used for any legal purpose until it has been admitted to "probate" by the proper court—which means that its genuineness and validity have been ascertained by the court. In numerous states a challenge to a will may be raised within a certain period even after the will has been admitted to probate. If the testator has failed to express himself with complete clarity, it may be necessary for the will to be "construed" judicially.

Will Substitutes

In order to avoid costs or pitfalls that may be connected with the making of a will, several types of transactions have evolved that are intended—in a less expensive and less awesome way—to take care of the transfer of property from one generation to the next. Among these "will substitutes," life insurance plays the most important role. Other methods of considerable significance are: (1) the revocable inter vivos (between living persons) trust; (2) the nomination of a third-party beneficiary in a government savings bond; (3) the creation of a joint tenancy in a piece of land, a bank account, or some other asset; and (4) the so-called tentative, or Totten, trust, whereby the depositor in a bank or savings institution designates a person who is entitled to withdraw whatever may be left in the account at the time of the testator's death. This "poor man's will" is popular in the state of New York, but its legal effectiveness has not been firmly determined in all of the other states.

The frequent resort to will substitutes in the United States perhaps indicates the desirability of a thoroughgoing revision of the overcomplicated American law of wills. Reliable statistics on the proportion of property owners dying testate (with a will) and intestate (without a will) would be desirable. But even today, such statistics are almost completely unavailable. Although the majority of adult persons seem to die intestate, it is also probable that wills cover the majority of the considerably smaller group of those leaving substantial estates.

IV. The Bench and the Bar

"The profession of law is the only aristocratic element which can be amalgamated without violence with the natural elements of democracy, and which can be advantageously and permanently combined with them."

—Alexis de Tocqueville

15.
Legal Education

The U.S. law school, as we think of it today, is little more than one hundred years old. The progress of American legal education has been slow, and it is only in the last fifty years that it has achieved the professional prestige it now enjoys.

At the time of the American Revolution, legal education consisted simply of apprenticeship in the offices of practitioners of law. Some practitioners' offices became schools; the most famous was that of Judge Tapping Reeve, established in Litchfield, Conn., about 1784.

Legal education in universities developed slowly. The first professorship of law was founded in 1779 at the College of William and Mary in Williamsburg, Va. Soon thereafter, lectures on law were being given in a few other colleges. The most influential were those of the American jurist James Kent, when he was a law professor at Columbia College in New York City. Like the lectures of Sir William Blackstone in England, Kent's lectures were published (*Commentaries on American Law*, 1826–30). The Harvard Law School, the oldest existing U.S. law school, was established in 1817, and several other universities established schools shortly thereafter. The method of instruction, which remained unchanged until the late 1880s, was a combination of lectures, textbook study, and quizzes. The textbooks often grew out of the lectures—as in the case of the notable series by Justice Joseph Story, who combined duties on the Supreme Court with teaching at Harvard.

Enriching the Curriculum

In 1870 the "case method" of teaching was begun at Harvard by Christopher Columbus Langdell. Its principal characteristic was the study of reported court decisions in the form of judicial opinions, instead of the usual texts or lectures. An accompanying characteristic, developed by Langdell's colleague James Barr Ames, was active class discussion, which began with close analysis of a specific case and ranged widely over hypothetical cases suggested by the students or teacher. The emphasis was more on the development of the students' analytical powers than on conveying information. By World War I the case method was being used in all major law schools, and it is still the primary teaching approach today.

In the 1920s several factors combined to bring the adequacy of the case method into question. One was the expansion of legislation and administrative law, with the development of new fields of great importance, such as taxation. Another was the growth of social science and the desire to make use of its findings in the law. Still another was the increasing interest in jurisprudence (the science or philosophy of law).

New theories of law developed, and legal institutions were reevaluated. The two main schools, if they may be called such, were sociological jurisprudence—with its functional approach, developed by Roscoe Pound at Harvard—and "legal realism," fostered by Karl Llewellyn at Columbia and other colleges. Both schools, particularly legal realism, were attempts to account for what many perceived as a massive breakdown in the system. Precise logic no longer seemed able to cope with changing social conditions. The answer of the legal realists appeared to be a call for a more candid study of judicial decision making and its inherent problems and limitations.

The result was that in the 1920s and 1930s, law schools developed enriched curriculums—their courses stimulated by questions from philosophy and the social sciences and their subjects reorganized to achieve a greater coherence. The casebooks were no longer only collections of cases, but they also contained text and nonlegal materials. The emphasis in class came to be less on the "correct" answer and more on an accurate identification of the legal issues and interests at stake.

At the same time teaching methods began to change. Emphasis was put on the firm handling of cases and problems as well as on the analytical and critical consideration of them. Increased attention was given to professional skills, such as counseling, drafting, and advocacy, or pleading a case. At times a problem method was employed that called for the consideration of new problems and their solutions. Although the prevailing system of instruction continued to be the case method in larger classes, undergraduate seminars and individual research came into use, and moot courts (assemblies for the argument of hypothetical cases) were found everywhere. The most distinctive form of independent student work was the law review. In the United States, unlike any other country, the learned journals of the profession are edited and produced by students in the law schools.

The "defense attorney" questions a young "witness" before the "judge" in a moot court trial. The argument of hypothetical cases in moot courts gives law students practical experience in professional skills.

Standards

Before World War II most law schools accepted all applicants who had the required amount of college work. A few schools developed selective admission programs based on college records and legal-aptitude test scores. After the war numerous schools joined in developing and using better tests and expanded their selective admission programs. The result was twofold: more students were rejected for admission, but of those entering fewer failed—only five percent compared with thirty-three percent before the changes.

Two unofficial bodies have influenced law school development—the Association of American Law Schools (AALS) and the American Bar Association. The AALS, organized in

1900, sets rules and standards for membership, and its annual meetings of law teachers and deans further the exchange of ideas on legal education. The American Bar Association, through appropriate membership sections, maintains a list of law schools that bear its stamp of approval. The standards of both associations have risen steadily. Neither the law schools nor the associations dictate the content of prelegal work, although the schools usually recommend college courses that emphasize verbal reasoning skills.

Specialization

Graduate instruction leading to the master's degree in law (LL.M.) or to the doctorate (S.J.D.) is available after the first, or bachelor's, degree (LL.B., or more commonly now, J.D.). Such study is undertaken by those who wish to specialize in certain technical fields, such as tax or labor law, and more particularly by those who wish to teach or pursue scholarly work in law.

There is an increasing complexity in the law—a rise of new subjects and a number of rapid changes caused by new legislation and court decisions. Such complexity has created the need for practicing lawyers to continue their legal education. And so a new type of graduate training course has emerged for the experienced practitioner. The programs offer concentrated work for a short period of time and are usually run by bar associations with the cooperation of law schools.

Preparing to Practice

In most states study in law school is the only legal training required of a person in order to take a bar examination and to be admitted to practice. No apprenticeship is required. A few states, notably Pennsylvania, have required a brief period of clerkship in a law office. Even though it is not required, an informal apprenticeship or association of a younger lawyer with older lawyers is common.

In many schools there have been efforts, through legal aid clinics, to bridge the gap between law school and the actual practice of law. Study in a law office as the method of preparation for admission to the bar has almost disappeared. In some areas a system of part-time law school study during the afternoons or evenings is available for those who must earn a living while studying. The period of law study for such part-time students is four years, compared with three years for full-time students.

Law and the Social Sciences

A striking characteristic of American law schools is their isolation from the other schools of a university. The liberal arts college developed its distinctive form before the law school appeared as part of the university, and law school work follows the completion of the student's work in college.

When the social sciences developed, they were not welcomed in the law school because of the professional, rather than academic, background of common-law study. This was true even of political science and economics, which are close to much of a lawyer's work. These subjects found their place outside the law faculty, not within it as in many countries, but the separation is lessening. Beginning in the 1930s, when Yale University, for example, asked an economist to teach a course in torts, law schools have been trying to integrate social science disciplines into the regular curriculum. In a few universities, professors of the humanities or of social sciences are on the law faculty. In others, members from the law and other faculties join in seminars or research to treat problems of common concern. Some courses on methods and processes of law are now being offered in undergraduate colleges by members of the faculties of law or of political science.

After the interruption caused by World War II, two distinct but complementary movements received increasing emphasis. One stressed the skills of the lawyer, identifying them more precisely and offering improved methods of developing them. The other movement was based on a broad view of a lawyer's function and opportunities and a clearer recognition of his or her professional and social responsibilities. The second movement, accordingly, sought to broaden the law curriculum. These movements were not new, but they gained strength from the larger role played by the government, the opportunities of lawyers in public service, and the magnitude and urgency of postwar problems. The rise of the public interest lawyer is a phenomenon undeniably linked with socially significant decisions of the Supreme Court during Earl Warren's chief justiceship (1953–69); it has helped galvanize the two movements. During the 1960s there was, correspondingly, a heightened concern for clinical education (education in neighborhood clinics that offer legal services for the indigent) and skills. These goals have received less emphasis in recent years, but U.S. legal education remains predominantly professional rather than academic in outlook and content.

16.
The Legal Profession

The legal profession is the vocation based on expertness in the law and its application. The two main divisions, by function, are the judges (the bench) and the practicing lawyers (the bar). Any discussion of the profession on a purely functional level, however, is apt to be somewhat misleading. The role of the lawyer, at least in the United States, far exceeds his technical skills.

Because of their training, contacts, or other reasons, lawyers are often placed in the position of being policymakers or executives in either industry or the government. Since the New Deal of the 1930s, for example, it has been common for many corporate lawyers, particularly in New York City and Washington, D.C., to spend large periods of their careers alternately in each field. As a result, the lawyer in America assumes a position of vast influence. The condition is especially worth noting, because it is almost unparalleled in other countries. Lawyers in England and France, for example, occupy a much more clerical role than do their American counterparts.

Functions and Standards

The primary function of the profession is to apply and utilize the law in specific cases—in short, to individualize the law. This function is manifest in the work of the advocates (lawyers who plead cases) and the judge in the courtroom, where cases are tried and decided. A lawyer will investigate the facts and the evidence by conferring with his or her client, interviewing witnesses and reviewing documents, and preparing and filing the appropriate pleadings (legal applications that advocate a cause) in court. The lawyer may seek a summary judgment because the opposing party evidently has no case, or through discovery proceedings he may force the other side to reveal more fully the issues and the facts on which it relies. At the trial he or she will introduce evidence, object to improper evidence offered by the other side, and argue questions of law and fact. If a lawyer loses, he or she may seek a new trial or relief in an appellate court.

Even in controversy, lawyers do more than press their cases to the end before the court. Negotiation, reconciliation, compromise—in all of which lawyers have a large part—bring about the settlement of most cases without a trial. Given the high costs of litigation—especially for "in-court" time— many lawyers feel that they have realistically lost their case if they have to proceed to trial.

In office work, too, the profession applies and utilizes the law. The lawyer may advise a client on the law and prevent a plan of dubious legality. In conference with the client and through negotiations with others he or she may aid in developing a wise plan to be embodied in a contract or other agreement. The law gives to private persons the power to arrange and determine their legal rights in many matters and in various ways, such as through wills, contracts, and corporate bylaws. In aiding these arrangements the lawyer is helping to particularize the legal rights of the parties.

Bert Lance is represented by his attorney, Clark Clifford, at a Senate hearing. The representation of clients before administrative commissions and legislative committees has become an increasingly important field in the legal profession.

Another field of work, which developed rapidly in the mid-twentieth century, is the representation of clients before administrative commissions and legislative committees. This development came about because of the increase in government regulation of modern life and the recognition of the importance of quasi-judicial bodies and their effect on legal rights and liabilities.

The lawyer is retained by one side only, even in office

matters, and is a partisan. The method of settling unresolved controversies is a competitive one—the adversary system of administration of law under which lawyers zealously represent their respective sides. This method involves a formidable paradox—the use of a partisan representative to bring out the truth and to achieve equal justice under law.

Lawyers, like other persons, have several loyalties in their work. These include loyalty to clients, to the administration of justice, to the community, to the associates in their practices, and to themselves—whether to their reasonable economic interests or to their own ethical standards as persons. These diverse and at times competing loyalties must be reconciled wisely and honestly. It is the purpose of the standards of the profession to bring about this reconciliation. For instance, a lawyer's loyalty to a client keeps him or her from representing someone else with competing interests. In the trial of a case a lawyer must be zealous but fair. The duty of fairness and candor is especially incumbent on the government's lawyer in a criminal prosecution. Of this duty the Supreme Court of the United States has said: "The United States attorney is the representative not of an ordinary party to a controversy, but of a sovereignty whose obligation to govern impartially is as compelling as its obligation to govern at all; and whose interest, therefore, in a criminal prosecution is not that it shall win a case, but that justice be done" (*Berger* v. *United States*; 1935).

The standard that most troubles laymen is the one that allows a lawyer to defend anyone accused of a crime. As a canon of the American Bar Association provides: "It is the right of the lawyer to undertake the defense of a person accused of crime, regardless of his personal opinion as to the guilt of the accused." The reason given is, "Otherwise innocent persons, victims of only suspicious circumstances, might be denied a proper defense."

Growth and Change

The history of the American legal profession goes back to England and to the profession that developed the common law there. In the United States, however, the English distinction between barristers (who argue in court) and solicitors (who do all legal work except courtroom arguments) has never taken root. In the simple life of the early colonies the need for lawyers was not obvious. As society became more complex, lawyers' work increased. Concern for family life and a need to enforce the criminal law were always present. With the development of a sovereign nation, other fields of practice became important. Land, commerce, industry and finance, taxation and government regulation—each, in turn, came to form a major share. The most pervasive change in the nineteenth century was the decline in the amount of advocacy and the increase in office work, which now makes up the bulk of law practice.

The late nineteenth century saw the rise of the lawyer, in terms of influence and prestige, to a position never before realized. As the Industrial Revolution reached full flower, and as government regulation of business began to reach significant levels, the need for expert legal advice of a high technical quality became acute. Leaders of the bar attained a new prominence. In the law, as in many other areas, the late nineteenth century was a "golden age."

Problems in the System

Dissatisfaction with the legal profession grew increasingly in the first third of the twentieth century. The bar lost its one-time leadership because it ceased to lead and to make social contributions commensurate with its political preeminence. In the first three decades of the century the judges—acting with a sense of duty but seldom guided by a liberal appreciation of expanding public interests—invalidated many popular legislative reforms. "Most of the common law has developed in that atmosphere of indifferent neutrality which has enabled courts to be impartial but also keeps them out of touch with vital needs" (Freund). Even the intelligent layman in America rarely knows anything of law except through the newspaper. There he reads only of constitutional questions, seemingly mere matters of public policy of which anyone may judge and which often seem irrational; of criminal cases that parade all the vices of criminal procedure; of crowded dockets and delayed justice in spite of judicial work schedules which—at least to the layman—appear leisurely indeed. Hence the discontent that precipitated earlier in the century a demand for the recall of judges and judicial decisions by popular vote. Other demands rose for limitations upon the power of divided courts to invalidate statutes. All of these demands became law in a few states. The administration of justice became a paramount problem of national life. The principal problems in civil cases were overcrowded trial dockets and reversals of trial decisions on very technical grounds. A good deal was accomplished eventually by a changed attitude on the part of the appellate judges, who ceased to order new trials for immaterial defects. Petty litigation in great urban centers was expedited and cheapened by the creation of simplified trial procedures (that is, small claims courts).

All the evils of procedure applicable to civil cases existed in a more aggravated form in criminal cases, with even more problems. It became clear that there was actual inequality among persons—rich or poor—before the law, because of its delays. In 1909 Pres. William Howard Taft declared that the administration of the criminal law in all the states (with possibly "one or two exceptions") was "a disgrace to our civilization." Delays in picking juries, in trials, and particularly in appeals all became critical during this period.

All of these evils—equally with trial and appellate courts, with civil and criminal cases—sprang from a deeply rooted attitude toward litigation as a mere game of wit. The only possible cure was through an increased power and awakened conscience of the bench and a higher moral tone of the bar. At least insofar as intellectual climate is concerned, there were improvements during the late 1920s and 1930s. The university law schools, led by the faculties of Columbia and Yale, attained excellence and a high professional prestige. Higher standards of education were enforced through requirements of admission to the bar of the states. Bar associations developed standards of ethics and professional conduct. The bar, in effect, appeared to clean its own house of attitudes that had brought it into disrepute. Internal housekeeping, however, did not solve all the problems: the availability of lawyers still depended to a large part on the ability of clients to pay, and criminal defendants were not universally assured of having a lawyer to represent them at trial until the Supreme Court decision of *Gideon* v. *Wainwright* (1963).

Admission to Practice

Each state grants qualified applicants the privilege of practicing law within its borders. The requirements for admission call for a bar examination (usually a two-day written test) preceded by three or four years of college and three years of legal education. Other requirements include approval of the applicant by a committee on character and fitness of the bar association. To practice in a federal court, a lawyer needs a grant of the privilege from that court, a decision based primarily upon previous admission to a bar of a state.

The exclusive nature of the lawyer's privilege to practice law raises questions of what tasks fall within that privilege. The questions have become urgent in the last two generations, with the rise of new experts who claim to provide expertise that the lawyer does not have—at least in the same measure—and of organizations that provide some services with seemingly greater efficiency and economy. The accountant in tax matters, the title company in sales of land, and the trust company in estate work are examples. Bar association committees formed to help prevent unauthorized practice of law have as their announced guide the protection of the public against persons who lack the intellectual qualifications and professional standards necessary for legal work.

Methods of Providing Legal Services

The traditional method of providing legal services is for the individual lawyer to be retained by and represent the individual client. As late as 1970 nearly two-thirds of the American lawyers in private practice practiced individually. However, the development of huge partnerships of lawyers has been stimulated by the growing complexity of the law. There are some very large partnerships, notably in New York City and Houston, with seventy-five to one hundred partners and one hundred to one hundred fifty other salaried lawyers. The law profession has not yet developed an adequate system of referral or consultation through which the general practitioner could obtain the aid of an expert when needed.

Large industrial corporations increasingly employ salaried lawyers who give full time to the company's work. The legal department of a large corporation handles almost all of the company's legal work and resembles, in both size and function, a small law firm.

Several methods are used to provide legal services to the poor. The oldest is the system of "assigned counsel," in criminal cases, with the court designating a lawyer to represent the accused. Another method is that of the public defender employed and compensated by the state or federal government to represent indigent defendants. A third method is that of legal aid societies. Legal aid organizations represent clients in civil and some criminal cases and are supported mainly by private donations, although the federal government has become more active in its support and more concerned with legal aid in recent years.

The lawyer reference service is for those who are able to pay a fee but do not know whom they should consult. The office of the service gives the inquirer a list of lawyers who are competent to handle his or her case. The lawyer will confer with the inquirer for a specified small fee and determine whether the case merits further attention and what the additional fee should be.

The question of fees and access to lawyers is likely to undergo substantial change in the next few years in the light of two decisions by the Supreme Court. In 1975 the Court opened the door for competitive fees by holding that uniform fixed fees set by bar associations violated the antitrust laws. Of greater importance is a 1977 decision holding that lawyers, like pharmacists and others, have a constitutional right to advertise their fees—at least for certain services; the decision (*Bates* v. *Arizona State Bar*) will undoubtedly mean that the public will become more aware of the variety of services that lawyers are able to provide and that the fees charged for such services will be subject to an open market.

The federal government, as well as the states, counties, and municipalities, has its own legal representatives. The chief law officer of the United States is the attorney general. As head of the Department of Justice he is a member of the Cabinet. He also is in charge of the United States attorneys, who represent the federal government in the district courts throughout the country. Second in importance in the Department of Justice is the deputy attorney general. The third-ranking member is the solicitor general, who is the government's lawyer before the Supreme Court.

17.
Legal Aid

Legal aid is professional legal assistance given, either free or for a nominal sum, to indigent persons in need of such help. In the United States there is a comprehensive network of autonomous legal aid societies, largely organized and financed through voluntary effort, which provide legal advice without cost (or for a very nominal fee). If necessary, they also provide representation in negotiations and in court to persons who do not have the means to pay lawyers' fees. Most are charitable corporations sponsored by bar associations, governed by community boards of directors, and supported by donated funds. A few are tax-supported bureaus.

In recent years the federal government has attempted to organize and partially fund neighborhood legal clinics, offering legal services for indigent clients. Service is generally rendered to clients by salaried staff lawyers and sometimes by volunteer lawyers in private practice. Organized legal service in criminal courts is provided largely because of decisions by the Supreme Court, which require that any person charged with a crime be represented by counsel if conviction of the crime could result in a jail term—even a brief one. Volunteer service committees of local bar associations operate in smaller communities not served by legal aid and defender offices.

Growth of U.S. Legal Aid

The legal aid movement in the United States began in 1876 when a group of citizens of German origin in New York City formed an office intended chiefly to assist German immigrants in the protection of their legal rights. By the time the organization had broadened the scope of its activities to serve all members of the community who were unable to pay lawyers' fees, a similar service had been organized in Chicago that undertook to give legal assistance to all persons without means, regardless of nationality, race, or sex. By 1916 there were forty-one legal aid organizations providing service in thirty-seven cities, five of them offering help in criminal cases.

A nationwide study of legal aid made in connection with a survey of the legal profession under the sponsorship of the American Bar Association (ABA) revealed that by 1949 there were ninety legal aid offices operating in eighty-three cities

A lawyer confers with her client in a legal aid office. Although litigation is sometimes undertaken, the services of legal aid offices are usually confined to providing assistance and advice.

and thirty-four public defenders' offices. The study also disclosed the vast extent of the need for more of these facilities. The ABA and various state and local bar associations accepted more responsibility for providing the movement with leadership and initiative. As a result, by the mid-1960s there were more than 230 legal aid offices in the country, about 115 public defender offices, and more than 125 volunteer service committees of bar associations.

Clients and Services

The work of legal aid offices is usually confined to providing assistance and advice to the very poor, which frequently means giving help to persons needing some sort of welfare, such as aid to families with dependent children (AFDC) or Social Security benefits. Little constitutional litigation is undertaken by such offices, although from time to time suits are filed to challenge statutes or regulations that affect welfare programs.

The bulk of constitutional litigation is undertaken by privately funded organizations whose main goal is to secure basic constitutional rights not only for the needy but also for members of the middle class who are able to afford lawyers but are not able to wage complicated litigation. National organizations such as the American Civil Liberties Union Foundation (ACLUF) and the Legal Defense and Education Fund of the National Association for the Advancement of Colored People (NAACP) are two prominent examples of such groups. In recent years specialized groups have emerged to undertake similar activities in more limited spheres; examples are the Environmental Defense Fund and the National Resources Defense Council. Smaller groups such as Public Advocates, Inc., in San Francisco, or the Southern Poverty Law Center in Montgomery, Ala., undertake similar tasks on a more local level. The ability of such groups to survive has been a function of their ability to win attorneys' fees in successful constitutional litigation. In 1974 the Supreme Court held that the award of such fees by federal courts was not permissible, but Congress enacted legislation in 1976 authorizing the award of fees in most civil rights legislation.

In an effort to add some degree of central direction in providing legal services for the poor, Congress enacted legislation in 1974 creating the Legal Services Corporation—a public quasi-official agency that disburses federal funds and provides guidelines for their use. The corporation's fiscal 1978 budget was $2.05 million for more than seven hundred offices throughout the country.

Increasing Public Access to the Law

Legal aid offices and public interest organizations are not the only means of providing legal services to those who cannot afford to retain lawyers themselves. Many labor unions and a number of companies have begun to provide group legal services for their members, and a number of prepaid legal service plans and legal insurance plans are under study.

The problem is not so much one of providing legal services for the indigent as it is of providing competent services for the middle and lower-middle classes, whose needs are substantial but whose means do not allow for sophisticated legal work. A large problem is informational: several studies show that most Americans are unaware of their legal needs until they are confronted with liabilities or sanctions resulting from their ignorance. Some of the problem can be attributed to the ever-increasing, complex governmental regulation of everyday life, but part of the problem—perhaps a large part—is a distrust of lawyers and the profession. High fees for apparently simple services, such as uncontested divorces or probate of estates, help to fuel this feeling.

One response, which has been tried in several jurisdictions in varying forms for some time, has been the small-claims court. In these courts persons with complaints about broken contracts or simple disputes that involve relatively small amounts of money are able to argue their cases under a simplified procedure. In many places, lawyers are prohibited from representing either side. These courts have not been a great success, however, because their powers are limited and because at least one party frequently is a company or collection agency with the expertise of a lawyer at its command.

Afterword:
Reform and the Future of American Law

The American legal system seems to undergo periodic crises of self-confidence. In 1906 Roscoe Pound of the Harvard Law School admonished the American Bar Association over "The Causes of Popular Dissatisfaction with the Administration of Justice." Dean Pound's speech was commemorated in 1976 by a conference in St. Paul, Minn., on the same topic.

Although today the "causes" may be different from what they were seventy years ago, the feeling remains that the legal system is failing to live up to its promise to deliver fair, speedy, and affordable justice. Today's causes of dissatisfaction, and thus the agenda for law reform in the near future, touch both substantive and formal issues.

Substantive Issues

The scope of criminal law is a constant source of concern for the members of the legal profession and for the public. In recent years law reform groups, both inside and outside the profession, have focused much of their attention on decriminalization; that is, they have sought to remove criminal penalties for various forms of behavior such as the private use of nonaddictive drugs, prostitution, and other so-called victimless crimes.

But perhaps a more important issue in the reform of criminal law is related not to definitions of criminal conduct but to sentencing. A wide variety of groups and individuals have tried to create standards for imposing criminal sentences to combat the appearance, and frequently the fact, of arbitrary terms of imprisonment. The American Bar Association and the federal judiciary have been the most active in addressing this problem.

Another major area of study has been what might loosely be called the social control of corporations. A number of individuals and groups have sought to create mechanisms and procedures to make corporations more responsive to their stockholders and more socially responsible generally.

Institutions such as schools, mental hospitals, and prisons have also attracted the close scrutiny of law reformers. Underlying such scrutiny, however, are conflicting philosophical as well as practical concerns. On the one hand, many reformers want to see institutions become more humane and more responsive to individual needs. On the other hand, the cost of reform, both financial and institutional, has made this increasingly difficult.

The concern over monetary cost needs no explanation. Many feel, however, that institutions such as prisons and mental hospitals should be reformed, if at all, by local governments and not by federal regulation—be it by decrees from federal bureaucrats or federal judges. In short, reformers disagree as to both the substance and the appropriate vehicles of reform. State and local autonomy, which was unfashionable during the New Deal and the 1960s, has once again become a respectable philosophical position.

Formal Issues

The "causes for popular dissatisfaction" with the legal system have not focused primarily on substantive issues, however; more people seem to be deeply concerned, and indeed dissatisfied, not with the law itself but with its machinery. Much of the work of the Follow-Up Task Force on the 1976 St. Paul conference was devoted to the development of alternative methods of resolving legal disputes.

Neighborhood "justice centers," small-claims courts, and arbitration and administrative agencies have been suggested as alternatives to the full-blown, adversary process of adjudication that has dominated the legal system. The idea is that judges, reacting to opposing lawyers, are ill-equipped or even unnecessary to solve a wide variety of disputes that occur in modern society. Underlying this notion, to some extent, is a profound concern for the cost of traditional lawsuits, in both time and money. Many Americans simply cannot afford lawyers' traditional services, and many cannot wait the two to seven years that it takes to litigate fully the average lawsuit.

Responses to these central problems have been twofold: long-range reformers, typified by participants in the St. Paul conference, have suggested drastic changes in the mechanisms of resolving disputes—essentially, "de-lawyering" such disputes wherever possible; but short-range reformers, perhaps skeptical of such drastic changes, have sought to increase access to the present system. Two of the most important recent developments have been the advent of advertising by lawyers (to make more members of the public aware of the availability of moderately priced legal services) and of pre-paid "legal insurance" plans, which operate much like health insurance plans. Many labor unions provide such insurance, and wider adoption of the insurance has been suggested.

Another problem—the issue of the competency of those who provide legal services—unites both types of reformers. Much attention has been focused lately on the question of whether many lawyers, particularly trial lawyers, possess the competency to handle the wide variety of complex legal issues and activities demanded of them. Some states now require periodic reexamination of lawyers' basic knowledge and skills. Some jurists, most prominently Chief Justice Warren Burger, have called for certification of lawyers in specialized fields—with their legal practice limited to those fields.

One fundamental problem touches every issue of law reform: the law is essentially a conservative profession. Lawyers, by definition, look to the past—prior cases, past customs and practices, and other precedents. Looking to the future without the baggage of the past is difficult for any lawyer, and law reform suffers, therefore, from a perspective that is, in a sense, inconsistent with its goal.

① 3/5 slaves counted as population in apportioning representation.

② also counted as property for taxes

BIBLIOGRAPHY

The New Encyclopaedia Britannica (15th Edition)

Propaedia: This one-volume Outline of Knowledge is organized as a ten-part Circle of Learning, enabling the reader to carry out an orderly plan of study in any field. Its Table of Contents—consisting of 10 parts, 42 divisions, and 189 sections—is an easy topical guide to the *Macropaedia*.

Micropaedia: If interested in a particular subject, the reader can locate it in this ten-volume, alphabetically arranged Ready Reference of brief entries and Index to the *Macropaedia*, where subjects are treated at greater length or in broader contexts.

Macropaedia: These nineteen volumes of Knowledge in Depth contain extended treatments of all the fields of human learning. For information on *Law in America*, for example, consult: Administrative Law; Agency, Law of; Air Law; Arbitration; Bankruptcy, Laws Concerning; Business Associations, Law of; Canon Law; Carriage of Goods, Law of; Chinese Law; Civil Law; Commercial Transactions, Law of; Common Law; Comparative Law, Study of; Conflict of Laws; Constitutional Law; Contracts, Law of; Copyright Law; Courts and the Judiciary; Criminal Law; Cuneiform Law; Egyptian Law; European Law, Medieval; Evidence, Law of; Family Law; Germanic Law; Greek Law; Health and Safety Laws; Hellenistic Law; Inheritance; International Court of Justice; International Law; Jury; Labour Law; Law, Western Philosophy of; Legal Education; Legal Ethics; Legal Profession; Maritime Law; Military Law; Mortgages, Law of; Natural Law; Patent Law; Primitive Law; Procedural Law; Property, Law of; Roman Law; Soviet and Socialist Legal Systems; Space Law; Tax Law; Torts, Law of; Trademark Law; Trusts, Law of; United Nations; War, Laws of; War Crimes; Welfare and Security Programs. For biographical and geographic entries, check individual names.

Other Publications:

American Jurisprudence; A Modern Comprehensive Text Statement of American Law, State and Federal. 2d ed., completely revised and rewritten by the editorial staff of the publishers. Rochester, N.Y.: Lawyers Co-operative; San Francisco, Calif.: Bancroft-Whitney, 1962–74. Kept up-to-date by supplements.

Black, Henry Campbell. *Black's Law Dictionary: Definitions of the Terms and Phrases of American and English Jurisprudence, Ancient and Modern.* Revised 4th ed., by the publisher's editorial staff. St. Paul, Minn.: West Publishing Co., 1968.

The Constitution of the United States of America: Analysis and Interpretation, Annotations of Cases Decided by the Supreme Court of the United States to June 29, 1972. Prepared by the Congressional Research Service, Library of Congress. Washington, D.C.: U.S. Government Printing Office, 1973.

Corpus Juris Secundum; A Complete Restatement of the Entire American Law as Developed by All Reported Cases. By Willaim Mach and Donald J. Kiser, assisted by the combined editorial staffs of the American Law Book Co. and West Publishing Co. Brooklyn, N.Y.: American Law Book Co., 1936–74. Kept up-to-date by cumulative annual parts and recompiled volumes.

Friedman, Lawrence M., and Scheiber, Harry N., eds. *American Law and the Constitutional Order: Historical Perspectives.* Cambridge, Mass.: Harvard

University Press, 1978.

Gaynor, James K. *Profile of the Law.* 4th ed. Washington D.C.: Bureau of National Affairs, 1978.

Legal Almanac Series. Dobbs Ferry, N.Y.: Oceana Publications, 1952-

U.S. Laws, Statutes, etc. *United States Code.* 1976 ed. Washington D.C.: U.S. Government Printing Office, 1977.

Picture Credits

Key to abbreviations used to indicate location of pictures on page: l.—left, r.—right;
—courtesy. Abbreviations are combined to indicate unusual placement.

Index

d

The Inquisitive Mind

Bantam Book Catalog

Here's your up-to-the-minute listing of over 1,400 titles by your favorite authors.

This illustrated, large format catalog gives a description of each title. For your convenience, it is divided into categories in fiction and non-fiction—gothics, science fiction, westerns, mysteries, cookbooks, mysticism and occult, biographies, history, family living, health, psychology, art.

So don't delay—take advantage of this special opportunity to increase your reading pleasure.

Just send us your name and address and 50¢ (to help defray postage and handling costs).